Seeing from the Summit

Seeing from the Summit

The Journey to an Effective Church

MARTY GUISE

LAY RENEWAL MINISTRIES

RESOURCE *Publications* • Eugene, Oregon

SEEING FROM THE SUMMIT
The Journey to an Effective Church

Copyright © 2011 Marty Guise. All rights reserved. Except for brief quotations in critical publications or reviews, no part of this book may be reproduced in any manner without prior written permission from the publisher. Write: Permissions, Wipf and Stock Publishers, 199 W. 8th Ave., Suite 3, Eugene, OR 97401.

Unless otherwise indicated, Bible quotations are taken from New International Version (NIV) of the Bible. Copyright (c) 1985 by Zondervan.

Resource Publications
An Imprint of Wipf and Stock Publishers
199 W. 8th Ave., Suite 3
Eugene, OR 97401
www.wipfandstock.com

ISBN 13: 978-1-60899-932-3

Manufactured in the U.S.A.

To my Lord and Savior, Jesus Christ
I breathe because He gave me life.

To Bob and Delores Fenn
who stepped forward in faith in 1954.

To Bob Fenn, Joe Schluchter and Tom Donner
*three incredible men who reflect Christ in ways
that continue to amaze me each day.*

To my beautiful bride, Diana
my treasure and support in countless ways.

To my children, Drew and Katie
you give me hope for the future.

Contents

Introduction / ix

1. Is there a Plan B? / 1

   TIER 1—MISSION / 7

2. Motivation / 12
3. Obedience / 34
4. Attitude / 51

   TIER 2—UNITY / 67

5. Relationships / 69
6. Communication / 85
7. Structure / 99

   TIER 3—DIRECTION / 123

8. Vision / 125

   Conclusion / 142

Introduction

As I stood at the base of the sheer cliff wall, I wondered how I could possibly reach the top. My older, stronger brother had attempted and failed a mere fifteen feet from the top. Was it worth the risk? Was it worth the shame I would feel if I failed?

I knew one thing. I had to try.

As I climbed the rock wall, I felt gingerly along the rock face—searching for solid places to place my fingers and toes. The encouragement shouted by my father challenged me to continue climbing. Eventually, I reached the same point as my brother. Was this the end? Would I be forced to return to the bottom unsuccessfully?

Moving along the wall, I felt a sliver of a crack. As I tested the area, I could feel it pulling loose. I called down "*Rock!*" as I swiftly moved out of the path of the large rock that broke free. I looked down as the thundering crash echoed in my ears and was grateful to see that everyone had been able to move safely out of the way.

As I looked back up, I realized that the fallen rock had left a tremendous hole that I was now able to use to finish my ascent! I swiftly completed the climb and gazed around joyfully at the view of the surrounding area.

* * * * *

In life and in ministry, there are those things that seem impossible. Things have been attempted and failed. Oftentimes, we are so close to the goal, but something seems to be stopping us from reaching that next point.

Since 1954, LRM has been working with churches and leadership to move forward as God directs. In 1996, I left seminary and my staff position at a local church to join Lay Renewal Ministries (LRM). I believed in the mission of the ministry then and I have seen it bear tremendous fruit over the years.

x   *Introduction*

As I have continued to serve through this ministry, the illustration of moving the rock and completing my goal has resurfaced many times. There are many churches that have incredible opportunities ahead of them. However, for whatever reason, they are unable to get around or move those barriers that impede their progress. If you are taking the time to invest yourself in this book, you must believe there are wonderful things ahead for the church you serve. Thank you for your courage.

Please understand that this book is not intended to provide a "magic" panacea program to follow. Rather, I hope that we are able to move together to present a process for developing a strategic and Scriptural model for intentionally training and motivating your church leaders in the work of the church. The challenge of building an effectively functioning church is immense. The roles of the pastors and lay leaders are keys to working the plan.

The mission and vision must be clear and direct if they are to be fulfilled. In a sense, every Christian has been tasked to work in the kingdom through the vehicle of the church. Our jobs are very different, but God calls each person to contribute to the work of building an effective church. Reading through this book and exploring the exercises both individually and as a team will help the reader to understand and embrace the work of the church. It is important and it is necessary.

The premise is this: the work of the church is extremely significant and we must be highly effective in carrying out that work. In reaching effectiveness, there are some check points along the journey that each church should have in place. It is my hope that you will use these checkpoints and teamwork exercises with the other leaders in your church. Each leader *and* church member should have their role clearly defined. If you are working as God has directed, you can achieve that which God has called you to do.

Before starting to climb, it is important to grasp the big picture of the journey ahead. When climbers set out, they typically have a base camp. A base camp is an established point of safety. In the work of the church, the base camp must be the Word of God. All things should begin with the Word and it should be the point to which we return if there are any questions along the way.

In the model of effective leadership training, the base camp is the launching point. Each of the following checkpoints and switchbacks will be explored in great detail in this book, but let's take a step back and look at the steps in the climb before us.

* * * * *

Mission is the first step out of base camp. Mission is established through the commandment (or Great Commission) of Jesus Christ found in Matthew 28:19–20.

Once the mission is understood, we ascend to our initial checkpoint. In order to be on the same page regarding terms, we define "checkpoint" as that point at which you stop and review your surroundings before moving ahead. At our checkpoints, we will be looking at a key component of an effective church. The desire is for you to reach greater understanding of this component so that you can move forward.

Our first such checkpoint is called Motivation. Attempting the journey for the wrong reasons will not lead you to the correct destination. The leadership must understand their common Motivation in Christ.

Ascending to the next point mandates looking at Obedience. Obedience requires a careful review of spiritual disciplines. It also requires pulling together those things (like prayer, Scripture intake, etc . . .) that properly equip the leader. The last checkpoint on this part of the ascent is called Attitude. No climber should attempt to continue forward without a strong attitude and outlook of success if they are following God's plan as defined and supported by Scripture. While this may seem unnecessary, our experiences spanning more than five decades have affirmed the benefits.

At this point, the church has now reached its first switchback. A switchback is a radical turn designed to allow for a safer and easier ascent. The reason a switchback is used in this model is to allow the leadership to come together and both celebrate the progress and refocus for the continuing journey. The first switchback is "Unity."

While pausing at the point of Unity, it is important to recognize that the leadership team must make a shift in focus. Motivation, Obedience and Attitude are all things that can be done individually. While those things can be greater if they are done with mutual sharing and accountability, the truth is that they must be first done by the person alone.

Progressing forward in Unity, the first checkpoint a team will reach is Relationships. At this point, leaders will seek to understand their individual and common points of intersection. This will apply to them personally while relating to one another and corporately as they relate to God.

The next stage reached is Communication. While it may seem that this should have been reached some time ago, we have truthfully just passed the midpoint of the ascent. It is vital that effective communication channels are in place with an understanding of what has gone before. Without achieving success in the checkpoints along the path of mission and agreeing in unity, communication channels will fail because the foundation is poor.

The sixth checkpoint is Structure. The importance of Structure cannot be overemphasized as leaders approach the next switchback and the final checkpoint. Structure is that which allows the leaders to organize and prepare for future progress. Team work is a vital element to progress from here.

Another switchback has been placed at this point in the effort. Direction is important because leaders must decide if they truly wish to continue moving forward. While it may sound strange to say, many churches do not wish to make any changes. BUT—if a church is willing to seek God's direction, they can do marvelous things for the Kingdom!

The sole checkpoint after establishing Direction is Vision. Vision is that which allows the church to progress forward as God has designed. Vision helps to identify where people are and moves them to where God wants them to be. If a church has successfully progressed through the preceding six checkpoints, they are able to see clearly those things which God is calling them to accomplish.

* * * * *

When a church is successfully able to define its vision to make disciples and go into the world, the journey has not ended. In fact, it has really just begun! By following the methods outlined at each checkpoint and switchback in this model, the church will have successfully managed to establish an incredible system from which will flow definable action areas for growth. The journey will be much smoother as you ascend.

Please also understand one additional key fact. There are no Lone Rangers in the church. When climbing, the best results are achieved when there is a team. One person may remain at base camp and tend supplies.

Another may hold a safety line. A third person may use his or her skills to go slightly in advance in order to set anchors in place for those following to proceed more easily. A true leadership team will need to work together to develop a common trust and respect for each other—and a common motivation for the task at hand. It really is an awesome blessing—just watch out for those loose rocks!

1

Is There a Plan B?

Why me? Is there anyone who has not asked that question? Sometimes we may wonder why good or bad things are happening in our lives. We may wonder why we are sick while another person is not. We may wonder why we kept our job while another was released. There are some things that don't seem to make sense when they happen to us.

Are you ready for another remarkable reality? God, in His mysterious wisdom, chose *man* to accomplish His plan on earth! It is beyond our human capacity to understand why the most powerful being in the universe and Creator of *all* things would select man—sinful, fallen, and defiant man—to do His bidding.

The mystery only continues to grow as we ponder why God would ordain THE CHURCH as the mechanism through which man is to accomplish His plan. It is enough of a challenge for each individual man and woman to discern and accomplish God's plan for his or her lives. How then, can people with their diverse personalities, multiple agendas, motives and expectations possibly be able to work together? There must be a better way!

There's not.

For all of its shortcomings, problems and mistakes, the church has persevered throughout the centuries. Regardless of the sometimes limited effectiveness and on-going challenges, it is still God's plan. If you believe that God does not make mistakes (and, by the way, He does not), then the Church is exactly the right tool to accomplish God's plan.

There is no Plan B.

There is hope. In His perfect wisdom, God has ordained that certain members of the church be called out to serve as leaders. He has detailed the criteria and the responsibilities for leadership in His Word. Scripture often uses the directionless wanderings of sheep to exemplify the need for leadership. Human beings also need shepherds. God's people need leaders to guide, nurture, protect and "grow them up." There is no higher calling. As leaders in the church, you must understand that the work is extremely significant, you must be highly effective and it will be totally fulfilling *if* you are working according to His plan.

Consider this: Over 500 years ago, a man had a plan. It was very specific and he was committed to the course. Christopher Columbus was determined to find a way to the Indies without the long journey southward. He had his plan and believed he would be able to change the world forever with a new route.

He failed.

In fact, he was a complete failure in regards to his "life work." Truthfully, Columbus never found the path he was determined to discover and died not knowing it was possible. However, with the benefit of hindsight, we can see that he found something which was much more significant and worthwhile. He discovered a "new" continent.

When *you* considered or accepted the call to be a leader in the church, what did you think you would accomplish? When I accepted my first leadership position, I honestly expected to change the face of the church and Christianity in the world. Why not? I could see things that needed to be changed. I could see areas to be improved in our church. I could see ways to reach out to the community. I could see how we could better serve our missionaries. I was incredibly excited and ready to get to work.

I failed.

How? That's for another book! More important to the issues being addressed in this book is WHY do so many of us fail as we seek to serve God through His vehicle, the Church? Consider the following axiom:

- God commissioned the Church for the purpose of changing the world.
- He promised us that He would empower us with what is needed to carry out the task.

- For the most part, the Church is not significantly impacting the world today.
- Therefore, we must not be appropriating all of the Power that God has promised to us.

Can it really be that simple? Is it possible that we are simply not fully using the Power that is available to us? I can't answer that question for your church. Consider what might be available. Ask yourself if you believe that you pray enough? Do your leaders pray enough? Are the people in your church praying? It's been said the best way to gauge a church's health is to count the number of people who attend the prayer meetings. This may be a way to gauge whether or not you are reaching out to do all that God has prepared with all that is available.

Take some time to analyze the reality of the axiom above and consider its ramifications for your church today. Christianity is crying out for leadership. How do we better appropriate God's promised power? How can we be more effective?

Leadership Effectiveness Training will be driven by this axiom. It will be driven to help you impact both your own life and the life of your church, community and the world. I failed because I believed I could do it. It is not something that I could ever do. However, through the power of Christ and the effective appropriation of the power He has promised us, *we* can do it.

* * * * *

As we study the map in front of us for making our churches more effective, the importance of the base camp necessary to insure ongoing health will be apparent. Wise leaders are always mindful of both the starting point and progress. Accordingly, they perform evaluations to make sure that the underlying base system of the church continues to be strong and healthy. The most effective progress is always built by a team of unified individuals working with a common plan.

In order to begin the process of planning, it is important to agree on some basic assumptions. We don't want to be like a climber who underestimates the climb and returns prematurely.

First of all, we must agree on the meaning of the word "church." The word church does not appear in the Bible until the writing of the New

Testament. Our word "church" comes form the Greek word, "ekklesia," which means "a people called out by God for a special purpose." We see it first in Matthew.

> *And I tell you that you are Peter, and on this rock I will build my church, and the gates of Hades will not overcome it.*
>
> Matthew 16:18

Considering this is the first time this word is made reference to in the Bible, that conversation at Caesarea Philippi is a pretty strong declaration about the church built on Christ. It is actually a fairly comforting one as well. First of all, Christ does the building. Our greatest design could not *begin* to touch on the awesomeness of His workmanship. He is also protecting us. His church is so strong that the gates of Hades and the surrounding idolatry cannot defeat it.

He does have a plan for the church. He chose each person who is a part of His church for a specific reason and a specific purpose in the church.

> *For we are God's workmanship, created in Christ Jesus to do good works, which God prepared in advance for us to do.*
>
> Ephesians 2:10

God has a specific plan for each church. The purpose statement of the church is clear.

> *Therefore go and make disciples of all nations, baptizing them in the name of the Father and of the Son and of the Holy Spirit.*
>
> Matthew 28:19

> *He said to them, "Go into all the world and preach the good news to all creation. Whoever believes and is baptized will be saved, but whoever does not believe will be condemned.*
>
> Mark 16:15–16

> *But you will receive power when the Holy Spirit comes on you; and you will be my witnesses in Jerusalem, and in all Judea and Samaria, and to the ends of the earth."*
>
> Acts 1:8

We are to tell the world about Jesus. The Church is to help equip disciples. God provides us with a model of the church through His Word in the book of Acts.

> *Those who accepted his message were baptized, and about three thousand were added to their number that day. They devoted themselves to the apostles' teaching and to the fellowship, to the breaking of bread and to prayer. Everyone was filled with awe, and many wonders and miraculous signs were done by the apostles. All the believers were together and they had everything in common. Selling their possessions and goods, they gave to anyone as he had need. Every day they continued to meet together in the temple courts. They broke bread in their homes and ate together with glad and sincere hearts, praising God and enjoying the favor of all the people. And the Lord added to their number daily those who were being saved.*
>
> Acts 2:41–47

We know, without a single doubt, that the early church was God's plan. Scripture records time and again countless individuals coming to a saving faith in Jesus Christ as they interacted with the members of that first church.

* * * * *

This is where it gets really interesting. The essential disciplines of the modern day church are no different than the disciplines of the first church. There are essential elements of ministry that must be included in our *actions* as a church. If any of those elements are missing or weak, we will not have the success that was experienced by the first church.

These essential elements include the following:

- Worship
- Prayer
- Relationship Building
- Preaching and Teaching
- Missions / Outreach
- Evangelism
- Stewardship
- Sacraments

While this is a generically-phrased list, each church must individually subscribe to its own essential elements with an appropriate emphasis on each. Leaders must be engaged in this process and it must be grounded in the Word. Leaders must be intentionally seeking and striving to accomplish God's purpose for their specific church.

There is no Plan B.

    Accept it.

        Work with it.

            Thank God for it.

Tier 1

Mission

Base Camp

Therefore go and make disciples of all nations, baptizing them in the name of the Father and of the Son and of the Holy Spirit, and teaching them to obey everything I have commanded you. And surely I am with you always, to the very end of the age.

Matthew 28:18–20

People need a mission, a purpose for existing. They need to be excited about what they are involved in to be truly successful. (Simply look at the amount of time corporate America spends on encouraging employees through posters hanging in the break room to extravagant company banquets for proof of this fact.) The healthy church needs to feel confident that it is squarely planted within God's will. When we feel that what we are doing is significant, we are willing to extend ourselves in working for that cause.

When we do not have direction, it is like not having a shepherd. Matthew 9:36 states, "*And seeing the multitudes, He felt compassion for them, because they were distressed and downcast like sheep without a shepherd.*" Many churches today are downcast and feel like sheep without a shepherd. Many pastors today are likewise downcast, feeling like they have lost their sheep.

The first step then, is *for leaders to understand God's mission for the church they have been called to lead.*

* * * * *

What is "mission?" The simplest definition for the word mission in the context of the church is *a specific task to which a person or group of people have been assigned.* Who is the person from whom we have received the assignment? Jesus Christ.

In Matthew 28:19-20, Jesus commanded His disciples to *"Go and make disciples of all nations, baptizing them in the name of the Father and of the Son and of the Holy Spirit, and teaching them to obey everything I have commanded you."* This commandment was given as Jesus' final earthly instructions to the Church.

The Church was tasked to take their understanding of the prophecies of the Old Testament fulfilled through Christ to the world and share salvation through Christ alone. Rather than remaining as citizens of Jerusalem and continuing their former ways, they were commanded to share this "new" truth (1st John 2:7-8). The Church was to love the Lord their God with all their heart, soul and mind and love their neighbors as themselves (Matthew 22:37-40) as they were "going" into the world to make disciples.

WHAT HAPPENED? THE WORLD WAS CHANGED.

Disciples were released. A disciple is a follower. A Christian disciple is a specific follower of Jesus Christ. The first disciples had a clear, distinct and radical purpose. They were to go out and share the Truth of Jesus Christ. In so doing, others would be drawn into this new covenant of grace and sealed with the sign of baptism. The new disciples would be taught to obey the words of Jesus and live out their faith. In so doing, they would also go and make more disciples. It was a very simple and direct plan. It should still be.

WHAT ABOUT TODAY? WHAT IS HAPPENING?

Jesus' command to "make disciples" has been watered down and lost by many in the Church. The "*ABC's*" of the Church have become *Attendance,*

Buildings and *Cash*. True disciplemaking has lost significance as churches become introverted.

WHAT DO WE DO?

The first priority must be to establish a proper base camp on the foundation of Scripture. In the establishment of Mission as the base camp, the church becomes missional in focus and outreach. Rather than being inwardly focused, the church views the community and world with "missionary eyes." Questions are asked like:

- How can we serve the community?
- What form of outreach is most needed?
- What are the hurts of the people around us?
- What can I do to make a difference with my neighbors?
- What does this church have to offer our neighborhood?

To be clear, missional churches do NOT ignore spiritual growth of those in the church. In fact, members of a missional church should want to grow stronger spiritually so that they can more effectively present the Gospel as they are serving. Maturity is a desired trait. As Paul admonished:

> *Then we will no longer be infants, tossed back and forth by the waves, and blown here and there by every wind of teaching and by the cunning and craftiness of men and their deceitful teaching. Instead, speaking the truth in love,* **we will in all things grow up into him who is the Head, that is, Christ.** *From him, the whole body, joined and held together by every supporting ligament, grows and builds itself up in love, as each part does its work.*
>
> Ephesians 4:14–16 (emphasis added)

This blending of spiritual growth and community focused outreach is vital to an effective church with a solidly built base camp.

Action Steps:

As you consider the following questions, think about what impact the answer would have on your church today. How would it impact your church tomorrow? In the corporate world, two questions effectively determine the purpose and success of any business: *What's your business?* and *How's business?* The church is not a business and should not be treated as such. However, let's rephrase and consider these questions:

1. What is your mission?

Why does your church exist? Can you find those points found in the Great Commission (Matthew 28:19–20) within it? What are the things that your church is intentionally seeking to accomplish?

_____

_____

_____

_____

2. How is your mission progressing?

How well are you doing these things?

_____

_____

_____

_____

3. How do these two questions apply to your church?

Do you have an intentional plan as church leaders? How will you accomplish it? The Components of the Effective Church will help you to answer and to act on these questions.

2

Motivation

Where's the Joy?

It was the last inning. Ahead by one run, the outcome of this game would determine which team battled for the championship. With one out, a runner on second and a new pitcher on the mound, the tension was incredible. First pitch—the runner on second breaks for third—it's a grounder to second. The second baseman bobbles it! After what seems like an eternity, he finds the handle on the ball and tosses it to first. The runner is out.

Oh no! The runner on second had rounded third and is about to tie the game. The first baseman fires a bullet to the plate. The catcher squeezes the ball and drops to cover the plate as the runner slides. Everyone looks at the umpire. He's out! The winning team jumps up and down in celebration as the parents stand and cheer.

Parents?

OK—so, it wasn't the World Series. It was my son's 10 year old baseball team. But as the team raced off the field, I saw *pure joy* reflected on their faces. From the bodies leaping in the air to the smiles stretching across their faces, it was a sight that brought joy to my heart.

* * * * *

Quite frankly, I don't see a lot of that joy when I look around—especially on Sunday mornings. I have had the opportunity to worship in churches in hot and humid Florida and desert-dry California. I've visited churches in tropical Hawaii and urban Pennsylvania. From Fargo, North Dakota to

New Orleans, Louisiana, I seen some of this nation's grumpiest Christians. "Dour" barely scratches the surface as a descriptor.

Perhaps the most surprising factor to consider is that this includes the "Sunday-morning-smile!" I'm sure you know what I mean. When our world is crashing down around us, we still manage to put a plastic smile on our faces and give the stock "I'm fine" when people ask how we are on Sunday mornings.

Let's go back to the foundation. What does God tell us about joy and its relationship to our first component—Motivation?

> *So David went down and brought up the ark of God from the house of Obed-Edom to the City of David with rejoicing. When those who were carrying the ark of the Lord had taken six steps, he sacrificed a bull and a fattened calf. David, wearing a linen ephod, danced before the Lord with all his might, while he and the entire house of Israel brought up the ark of the Lord with shouts and the sound of trumpets.*
>
> 2 Samuel 6:12b–15

If you didn't smile when you read that passage, take a minute to read it again please—and when you do, really put yourself into the passage. Imagine the rejoicing faces all around you. God was returning to the City of David! Imagine the sight of David as he danced WITH ALL HIS MIGHT. Sweat is flying everywhere. Arms are raised in praise. Open your ears to the sound of trumpet blasts and shouts! People are bursting with joy! I hope you are smiling now.

I hate to do this to you, but let's consider the next passage as we learn that Michal, daughter of Saul, is not joining in the celebration.

> *As the ark of the Lord was entering the City of David, Michal daughter of Saul watched from a window. And when she saw King David leaping and dancing before the LORD, she despised him in her heart. ... Michal ... said, "How the king of Israel has distinguished himself today, disrobing in the sight of the slave girls of his servants as any vulgar fellow would."*
>
> 2 Samuel 6:16, 20b

Talk about a splash of cold water on your face. Michal did not join "the entire house of Israel," but rather "watched from a window." David's reply to her is immediate and honest:

> *It was before the LORD, who chose me . . . I will celebrate before the LORD. I will become even more undignified than this and I will be humiliated in my own eyes.*
>
> 2 Samuel 6:21b–22a

David's motivation was pure and clear. David's motivation was joyful celebration that had grown out of his love and gratitude of being chosen by the Lord. His life became a literal dance before the Lord as he was compelled by the knowledge of the One who gives us life.

As you look at your own *church life*, is your motivation for serving as a leader more like that of a David or Michal? Are you able to gladly leap and dance for joy when called upon to prepare the budget? To fix a leaky toilet? To visit someone in the hospital?

> *For Christ's love compels us, because we are convinced that One died for all, and therefore all died. And He died for all, that those who live should no longer live for themselves but for Him who died for them and was raised again. So from now on we regard no one from a worldly point of view. Though we once regarded Christ in this way, we do so no longer. Therefore, if anyone is in Christ, he is a new creation; the old has gone, the new has come! We are therefore Christ's ambassadors, as though God were making his appeal through us. We implore you on Christ's behalf; be reconciled to God.*
>
> 2 Corinthians 5:14–17, 20

We are no longer our own. We live not for ourselves, but *for Him who died*. Therefore, our motive is now to live our lives for Him as His ambassadors in the world. Wow! God has specifically chosen you to be His special emissary to accomplish a great work for Him. He has also promised to empower you to accomplish this task.

In light of this, we must be very careful to guard our motivation. The temptation to allow pride to enter our hearts is constant. Our motivation must be driven by God rather than men. If we do what we want to do to look good before men, our motives are wrong (see Matthew 6:1). Our motive should be to please God rather than man. Consider this early example:

> *In the course of time Cain brought some of the fruits of the soil as an offering to the LORD. But Abel brought fat portions from some of the firstborn of his flock. The LORD looked with favor on Abel and his*

offering, but on Cain and his offering he did not look with favor. So Cain was very angry, and his face was downcast."

Genesis 4:3–5

God knows the heart and the motivation. Both Cain and Abel brought offerings to God. Abel's offering was accepted with favor. Cain's offering was not. The difference is that Abel brought his best to God. Our motivation should be to give our best to God in all that we say and do.

GUIDING PRINCIPLE

Pure motives in ministry are grounded in shepherds who do what they do because of an unquenchable love for Christ and who desire only to see the glory of God enhanced and His Kingdom advanced.

—Joseph Stowell

THE CHALLENGE OF LEADERSHIP

Leaders in the church are influenced by the component of motivation based on two principles. These principles are:

1. There is a Biblical model for proper and true motivation for serving.
2. Leaders must prayerfully create an environment in the church that God will use to motivate others to seek Him and grow in Him.

In addressing those two principles as leaders in the church, we need to ask the following questions.

- Why must we, as individuals following Jesus Christ, serve God?
- Why is it important for Christians to be motivated for service together through their churches?

- Who ultimately motivates us in our Christian walk?
- What responsibility does the church's leadership then have for the motivation of the body of Christ?
- Who is the focus of our motivation?

Moving through a discussion of these questions and then working through the exercises will help both you and the other leaders in your church to personally discover and then embrace an attitude of motivation that flows out of loving appreciation for the One who has given all. This attitude will reflect out to others a motivation that will encourage them to serve as Christ has called them to do.

As with each of the Checkpoints, we will look to God's Word for a Biblical model of these practices. While no one is perfect, we will seek guidance from Scripture to hear how God is speaking through these men and women. As we consider motivation, we will continue to explore David's life and the people surrounding him.

WHY MUST WE, AS INDIVIDUALS FOLLOWING JESUS CHRIST, SERVE GOD?

Let's take a step back to the first time we meet David. Samuel, Israel's last judge, had a difficult job. After the nation insisted on an earthly king, Samuel anointed Saul. Saul had physical characteristics that helped him to stand out physically as the "warrior king" the *people* desired (1st Samuel 9:2; 10:23). However, we see in Saul's life that serving the Lord was not his first priority. God then told Samuel that he was to anoint another whose *heart* was connected to Him. To find that person, we jump ahead to chapter 16.

Place yourself in the scene as an elder of the town. Samuel, the mighty man of God and prophet for the Kingdom appears coming up the road. The whispering you'd last heard was that he had gone to his home in Ramah after an argument with Saul. Your reaction most likely would have been the same response as the other elders in Bethlehem. Fear!

> *Samuel did what the LORD said. When he arrived at Bethlehem, the elders of the town* **trembled** *when they met him. They asked,* **"Do you come in peace?"**

1 Samuel 16:4 (emphasis added)

For the prophet of God to come knocking on your door was a bit surprising to say the least. What dire prophecy would he have? Had someone in the town sinned? What word would he bring from the Lord? What was going on with Saul? Was trouble coming?

Have you *personalized* that thought? For me, it brought to mind my probable response if my pastor or one of the leaders of my church came to *my* door. I would be wondering what I did wrong or what tragedy had transpired! At the very least, I would be quite anxious.

The point of this exercise is this—while we may have a reverential fear of an omnipotent God, we don't serve Him out of fear. That must be eliminated as an answer to the question of why we serve God. Fear may detract from service rather than add to it.

So, if fear is not the answer, what is? Let's jump back into the scene. Jesse's sons are coming in to be consecrated for the sacrifice. Eliab passes before him and, based on his appearance, Samuel thinks he will be the one. Watch and listen . . .

> *But the LORD said to Samuel, "Do not consider his appearance or his height, for I have rejected him. The LORD does not look at the things man looks at. Man looks at the outward appearance, but the LORD looks at the heart." . . .*
>
> *Jesse had seven of his sons pass before Samuel, but Samuel said to him, "The LORD has not chosen these." So he asked Jesse, "Are these all the sons you have?" "There is still the youngest," Jesse answered, "but he is tending the sheep." Samuel said, "Send for him; we will not sit down until he arrives." So he sent and had him brought in. He was ruddy, with a fine appearance and handsome features. Then the LORD said, "Rise and anoint him; he is the one."*

1 Samuel 16:7, 10–12

Out of eight sons who passed before Samuel, God chose David. Why? God saw David's heart. God knew that David was a man who truly loved Him and desired to serve Him with his life. It wasn't anything that David did. It wasn't anything about his appearance. To paraphrase, God said, "*He's mine.*"

And David went back to being a shepherd. But he was a shepherd with a mission. We'll talk more about that soon . . .

* * * * *

So, did we answer the question of why we must serve God? Let's step from the life of David to a passage from the letter of Paul to the church in Corinth.

> *For Christ's love compels us, because we are convinced that one died for all, and therefore all died. And he died for all, that those who live should no longer live for themselves but for him who died for them and was raised again.*
>
> 2 Corinthians 5:14–15

During his life, David did not meet Christ in the flesh. In fact, David's reign as king was over a 1,000 years before Jesus began His earthly ministry! So, what is the parallel?

Jesus died for all.

As David and the people of Israel went through the process of offering sacrifices, they knew that someday there would be a Redeemer. And so, they served God. Not perfectly of course, but in their day to day lives, they lived out their faith in loving appreciation for what God had done for them. He rescued them out of a land of slavery. He led them to the Promised Land. He broke down the walls of Jericho and gave His people an inheritance. Time and time again, the people wandered from God and then returned when the burden was too much. Then they served Him again. Why?

Loving Appreciation

Those two words are the best and most direct answer for why we serve God.

* * * * *

Tape four little words from 2nd Corinthians 5 on your alarm clock. When the alarm goes off in the morning, read those words and get out of bed. Tape them to the dashboard of your car and, as you are fighting traffic on the way to work, read those four little words. As you sit at your desk at work, read those four little words that answer the question *"Why?"* What are those words? *For Him who died.*

As a result of the sacrifice of Jesus Christ on the cross, the curtain has been torn and we can now approach our Heavenly Father. It is surrender and a response of loving appreciation that drives us to service and sustains us in our efforts.

Why is it so important to have a strong understanding of this principle? If the core people (including the pastor(s), staff and leadership team) involved in an effective church *and* the members of the congregation are properly motivated to serve the Lord Jesus Christ through His lordship, there is tremendous strength. This community of brothers and sisters in Christ are doing what they do through their church based on the same desire to be a missional band of believers sharing the Truth so they may honor and glorify God.

Motivation is the cornerstone of healthy church effectiveness. The proper motivation for Christians is a loving appreciation to a loving God. Unhealthy churches are those where members serve based on obligation or "duty." Healthy churches have leaders and members who desire not only to see people saved from sinfulness, but who would also call others to serve Him through His church. God's grace is a bigger concept than our finite minds are able to fully comprehend. However, as we daily seek and strive to understand the immensity of what God has done for us through Jesus Christ, we can begin to serve Him based on the proper motivation—loving appreciation.

Don't become nonchalant about your relationship with God. We must not take our spiritual inheritance for granted. It is important that, as we walk with the Lord and grow in our spiritual lives, we constantly remember *Him who died.*

David didn't go running to Saul and command him to step down from the throne. After being anointed by the prophet Samuel, David went back into the fields. From that day on, the Spirit of the Lord came upon him in power (verse 13). He continued his life of simple service until God opened the next door.

Reflect for a moment on the fact that God does love you. Yes—you. He loves YOU.

Let's respond by *serving* Him in love.

WHY IS IT IMPORTANT FOR CHRISTIANS TO BE MOTIVATED FOR SERVICE THROUGH THEIR CHURCHES?

Is that really the story? David gets called in from the field, anointed by the great prophet Samuel and then goes back to the sheep? What happened to his becoming king? And wait a minute—Saul was still the king! There could only be one king and now, unbeknownst to anyone outside of Jesse's household, Israel had two.

As we've said, David did not run to find Saul and tell him to step down. As evidenced throughout the rest of 1st Samuel, David tried to honor Saul as king in all things. Even when Saul sought to kill David and opportunities presented themselves to David on *multiple* occasions to respond by killing Saul, David restrained himself to seek God's direction. (See especially 1st Samuel 24:3-4. How would you like it if your tombstone stated that you were killed while going to the bathroom?)

As we consider the importance of motivation in relation to service through the church, I find it interesting to reflect back on the first time we met Saul. In chapter nine, we first encounter Saul as he sets out on a quest to gather—no, not sheep—donkeys!

Moses met God on Mount Horeb while shepherding the sheep. David was called from shepherding sheep to be anointed. Jesus is the Good Shepherd who watches his sheep. Saul knew how to take care of donkeys.

Consider the temperament of donkeys. They are known for being stubborn and difficult. I read a description of a donkey that stated they were self-preserving in nature. In simple language, *a donkey will do what is good for a donkey*.

Consider the temperament of Saul. In chapter thirteen, we see him sin against God by impatiently offering sacrifices without Samuel. In chapter fourteen, he is ready to kill his son, Jonathan, for eating to regain strength during battle. In chapter fifteen, Saul ignores the Lord's clear instructions. Samuel tells him:

> *"Does the LORD delight in burnt offerings and sacrifices as much as in obeying the voice of the LORD?* **To obey is better than sacrifice,** *and to heed is better than the fat of rams. For rebellion is like the sin of divination, and arrogance like the evil of idolatry. Because you have rejected the word of the LORD, he has rejected you as king."*
>
> 1 Sam 15:22-23 (emphasis added)

Saul did what was best for Saul.

As shepherds of God's flock, leaders must do what is best for the Kingdom. An individual church working together for God's glory can have an incredible witness to the world of the grace, mercy and love of lives transformed through the love of Jesus Christ.

Do you agree? Let's consider a few things before you decide.

In many churches we hear of the practice of the 80–20 Principle. 80% of the work is done by 20% of the people. Scripture is clear that we are called to be a community of believers. We are brothers and sisters in Christ. Therefore, we are *ALL* to work *together* to accomplish His plans. The Christian life cannot be a solitary journey. It is to be a group endeavor.

> *It is He who gave some to be apostles, some to be prophets, some to be evangelists, and some to be pastors and teachers, to prepare God's people for works of service, so that the body of Christ may be built up until we all reach unity in the faith and in the knowledge of the Son of God and become mature, attaining to the whole measure of the fullness of Christ.*
>
> Ephesians 4:11–13

The Bible makes it clear that all Christians have a role through works of service to build up the Body in unity, knowledge and maturity. We have all been given gifts that are crucial to the success of this thing we call the Church. And, even more specifically, leaders are called to equip and prepare the Church. Church leaders are called to activate and engage His chosen to make sure that all of the God-given human resources are contributing to the advancement of the Kingdom based on each believer's specific gifts.

Business projects fall short due to a variety of reasons. There may not be enough money. There may not be enough personnel assigned to the task. The deadline is too tight. The wrong systems were used. The list can go on and on. The question for the church is simply this: "Would God give you a job to do and not give you the means to do it?"

Let me give an example of a discussion I had with a group of leaders at a small church. During our time together, I learned they had not had a visitor in seven months. As we discussed some of the options for funding outreach, a leader shared that he was already giving to various groups outside the church. He had no additional money and he was not going to stop supporting those places. After learning that one of those organizations was a group that conducted heart research, I thanked him. My grandfather, father and brother have all had heart issues. But then, seeking to use that as an example, I took the group on a discussion of what would happen if—rather than writing a check to a heart research fund—each person would contribute some time and treasure towards a "Heart Fair" outreach event to be held at the church.

The leaders would contact local businesses, including a drugstore (on the other side of the parking lot), an exercise facility (down the street) and a hospital (less than a mile away). They would seek doctors, nurses, pharmacists, physical therapists, exercise experts, etc . . . who would occupy various booths around the church parking lot and share about heart health. A local sandwich shop (around the corner) that promoted healthy eating would be contacted to distribute coupons in order to encourage this practice. In addition, the church would have several outreach booths featuring balloons and other activities for children.

The central booth would be dedicated to spiritual heart care. The pastor or a leader in the church would be available to speak with people about spiritual needs. Tracts would be distributed and possibly a devotional booklet. Through this event, the church would have an opportunity to minister to those in the community on both a physical and spiritual level.

Let me be clear. This does NOT mean that everything we do must be done through the Church. An individual church cannot serve everyone, everywhere in every possible way. A person may have a wonderful and powerful ministry through which they are serving at the workplace or his or her neighborhood. In fact, as one simple example, Christian history is filled with people doing great things for God on the mission's field.

My argument is simply this: *Much more can be accomplished through the Body of believers working cooperatively than can be accomplished through our working independently.* A missionary supported by a church can be stronger through a true partnership. An individual serving through his or her workplace can be better equipped if other people are offering counsel and support. We are NOT merely called to serve Christ as individuals.

Therefore, the following statement could change the entire paradigm of leadership in the vital local Christian church. It establishes what the church is to be and how leaders are critically responsible for molding local church bodies into powerful tools for God's use. This statement empowers the effective church by challenging leaders to engage God's workforce, the priesthood of believers.

> God created the Church. He has a mission and vision for each congregation that He calls. The responsibility of church leaders is to discern what that mission and vision are and to discover, develop and deploy the resources that the congregation has been given. This includes time, talent and treasure. Each church requires the entire body of Christ to be involved to fully accomplish God's plan. By intentionally and vigorously shepherding the Body, Christian leaders will be used by God to activate a church, which will glorify Him as it accomplishes His will.

As you unpack and digest that thought and consider its components, what are the ramifications for you and your leadership team?

WHO MOTIVATES US IN OUR CHRISTIAN WALK?

I once attended a worship service in which the guest speaker brought a basketball, a football and a volleyball. As we walked out of the church that morning, I remember being very excited. Honestly, I could not tell you anything about the message, but I know the Body was excited. As I thought about it later, I was impressed with the speaker's ability to motivate the listeners. Is that real motivation though? If not, then how are we motivated to serve in our Christian walk?

As we look again at David, we see a tremendous example of fear turning into passion in his encounter with Goliath.

> *Now the Philistines gathered their forces for war and assembled at Socoh in Judah. They pitched camp at Ephes Dammim, between Socoh and Azekah. Saul and the Israelites assembled and camped in the Valley of Elah and drew up their battle line to meet the Philistines. The Philistines occupied one hill and the Israelites another, with the valley between them.*
>
> *A champion named Goliath, who was from Gath, came out of the Philistine camp. He was over nine feet tall. He had a bronze helmet on his head and wore a coat of scale armor of bronze weighing five thousand shekels; on his legs he wore bronze greaves, and a bronze javelin was slung on his back. His spear shaft was like a weaver's rod, and its iron point weighed six hundred shekels. His shield bearer went ahead of him.*

> Goliath stood and shouted to the ranks of Israel, "Why do you come out and line up for battle? Am I not a Philistine, and are you not the servants of Saul? Choose a man and have him come down to me. If he is able to fight and kill me, we will become your subjects; but if I overcome him and kill him, you will become our subjects and serve us." Then the Philistine said, "This day I defy the ranks of Israel! Give me a man and let us fight each other." On hearing the Philistine's words, **Saul and all the Israelites were dismayed and terrified.**
>
> 1 Samuel 17:1–11 (emphasis added)

As you read through the Old Testament, you will see a variety of approaches by Israel's enemies who seek to incite fear and surrender in the hearts of God's people. In one instance, the king of Assyria challenged God's protection and provision.

> "Say to Hezekiah king of Judah: Do not let the god you depend on deceive you when he says, 'Jerusalem will not be handed over to the king of Assyria.' Surely you have heard what the kings of Assyria have done to all the countries, destroying them completely. And will you be delivered? Did the gods of the nations that were destroyed by my forefathers deliver them: the gods of Gozan, Haran, Rezeph and the people of Eden who were in Tel Assar? Where is the king of Hamath, the king of Arpad, the king of the city of Sepharvaim, or of Hena or Ivvah?"
>
> 2 Kings 19:10–13

Rather than argue, Hezekiah went to the temple of the Lord and prayed to God.

> Hezekiah prayed to the LORD: "O LORD, God of Israel, enthroned between the cherubim, you alone are God over all the kingdoms of the earth. You have made heaven and earth. Give ear, O LORD, and hear; open your eyes, O LORD, and see; listen to the words Sennacherib has sent to insult the living God.
>
> 2 Kings 19:15–16

If you read the passage in Samuel closely, you may have noticed that Goliath identified the Israelites as "servants of Saul." While this may not seem important at first glance, when we see David's response to Goliath, we witness an important distinction.

Motivation: Where's the Joy?

> *David said to the Philistine, "You come against me with sword and spear and javelin, but I come against you in the name of the LORD Almighty, the God of the armies of Israel, whom you have defied. This day the LORD will hand you over to me, and I'll strike you down and cut off your head. Today I will give the carcasses of the Philistine army to the birds of the air and the beasts of the earth, and the whole world will know that there is a God in Israel. All those gathered here will know that it is not by sword or spear that the LORD saves; for the battle is the LORD's, and he will give all of you into our hands."*
>
> 1 Sam 17:45–47

David told Goliath that he was part of the army of the LORD Almighty. He wasn't coming to avenge Saul. He was coming to defend the honor of the God of Israel. Our motivation in service is to honor and glorify God out of loving appreciation for the gift of His grace and mercy.

Please don't misunderstand. I am not trying to promote a "works-based" salvation nor am I seeking to claim that God needs us to defend Him. Neither is true or necessary.

We must recognize that we serve God through the church as we are reaching a lost and dying world. We have been commanded by Jesus Christ to go into the world (Matthew 28:19–20) and share God's Truth and Love. We need to do that bravely—in assurance that God is with us.

How can we have the strength and courage that David had? It is impossible. Unless . . .

. . . unless we have the Holy Spirit.

The Holy Spirit motivates believers to Christian service through the church. God uses people as His instruments to help others understand the greatness of His love for us. Motivation then is proactive. As we learn more about God's love and begin to better comprehend it, we act in response to that love.

Is your church a place that encourages and enhances the work of the Holy Spirit? Is it winsome and holy? Is it active and alive? Is it inviting? Is it an environment that causes an outsider to be intrigued with its spiritual essence? Is it clear that there is something special going on there? As we are considering the Components of the Effective Church, we are considering how we might consistently position churches for God's most impactful use of them. Did any of the preceding questions make you wonder about your own church?

Again, consider the example of David and his audacity as he stood before Goliath. While he should have been trembling with fear like the rest of the Israelites, he stood strong and unflinching. He had the courage to act in the Strength of the Lord.

The pastor and the leadership of your church must have that same courage to act in God's strength. The pastor shoulders the primary responsibility as God's conduit for motivating the flock over which he or she is the shepherd. The most effective method for motivating people to come to Christ initially and to continue to seek Him is the steadfast preaching and teaching of the Word. As people understand the truths of the Scriptures, they will be motivated to serve Him fully with their lives.

> *Consequently, faith comes from hearing the message, and the message is heard through the word of Christ.*
>
> Romans 10:17

Each leader in the church must also have the same approach and steadfast resolve to teach and share the love and knowledge of Christ. This boldness will be a tremendous testimony to the church and will outflow to the community. Remember how both the Philistines and the Israelites responded to David's faith and example.

> *David ran and stood over him. He took hold of the Philistine's sword and drew it from the scabbard. After he killed him, he cut off his head with the sword.* **When the Philistines saw that their hero was dead, they turned and ran. Then the men of Israel and Judah surged forward with a shout and pursued the Philistines** *to the entrance of Gath and to the gates of Ekron. Their dead were strewn along the Shaaraim road to Gath and Ekron.*
>
> 1 Sam 17:51–52 (emphasis added)

The Philistines put their faith in a man. When he failed, they ran. David put his faith in God and God won. The Israelites responded by putting their faith in the God behind a man. The Israelites emerged victorious when they embraced God's Power.

WHAT RESPONSIBILITY DOES THE CHURCH'S LEADERSHIP HAVE FOR THE MOTIVATION OF THE BODY OF CHRIST?

As we look at the responsibility of the church's leadership, let's take another few moments to contrast Saul and David.

> *Goliath stood and shouted to the ranks of Israel, "Why do you come out and line up for battle? Am I not a Philistine, and are you not the servants of Saul? Choose a man and have him come down to me. If he is able to fight and kill me, we will become your subjects; but if I overcome him and kill him, you will become our subjects and serve us." Then the Philistine said, "This day I defy the ranks of Israel! Give me a man and let us fight each other." On hearing the Philistine's words, Saul and all the Israelites were dismayed and terrified. . . . Now the Israelites had been saying, "Do you see how this man keeps coming out? He comes out to defy Israel. The king will give great wealth to the man who kills him. He will also give him his daughter in marriage and will exempt his father's family from taxes in Israel." David asked the men standing near him, "What will be done for the man who kills this Philistine and removes this disgrace from Israel? Who is this uncircumcised Philistine that he should defy the armies of the living God?" . . . What David said was overheard and reported to Saul, and Saul sent for him.*
>
> 1 Samuel 17:8—11; 25—26; 31

Scripture is careful to point out that *both* Saul and all the Israelites were terrified of Goliath. They listened to this audacious taunt for forty days. In contrast, when David overheard Goliath's challenge and the Israelites' response, he became upset on his first day in camp. David wonders: *How dare these Philistines defy God?*

The word quickly gets around that there may be someone who is willing to take up the challenge against Goliath. Where was Saul? (To be more precise, where had he been for the past 40 days?) Saul was in his tent. He was not dressed in his armor ready to go to battle.

I'll never forget the inspirational scene in the movie *Braveheart*. In this film, William Wallace (played by Mel Gibson) appears with a small group of men in the midst of a massive desertion. With an inspirational speech and a bold challenge to the men, he turns them into a fierce group of warriors—ready to fight against a superior foe. If it had been possible, I would have leapt onto the screen myself with sword in hand!

But I've also stood in the Valley of Elah where this battle took place. I have imagined walking down to the middle of the Valley, away from those who could help me and closer and closer to danger. Each step closer to risk can be daunting. Each step is necessary.

Recognize this: *Leaders need to lead.*

Saul was in his tent. Rather than doing any number of things, he chose to do nothing for *forty* days. Imagine if Saul had stepped forward and boldly proclaimed "Even if I die, I will not have the name of God slandered!" (See Daniel 3:16–18.)

President Theodore Roosevelt was a leader who was a man of action. As a soldier, he was instrumental in the battle of San Juan Hill. As a president, he boldly proclaimed the necessity of our country to act against oppression. As a man of faith, he clearly declared the necessity of putting feet to faith. Listen to the words from a speech he gave at Trinity Reformed Church in Chicago in early September of 1901.

> *We must be doers—not hearers only. I am sure every one who tries to be a good Christian must feel a peculiar shame when he sees a hypocrite, or one who so conducts himself as to bring reproach upon Christianity. The man who observes all the ceremonials of the laws of the church but who does not carry them out in his daily life, is not a true Christian. To be doers of the Word it is necessary that we must be first hearers of the Word. Yet attendance at church is not enough. We must learn the lessons. We must study the Bible, but we must not let it end there. We must apply it in active life. The first duty of a man is to his own house. The necessity of heroic action on a great scale arises but seldom, but the humdrum of life is with us every day. In business and in work, if you let Christianity stop as you go out of the church door, there is little righteousness in you. You must behave to your fellowmen as you would have them behave to you. You must have pride in your work if you would succeed. A man should get justice for himself, but he should also do justice to others. Help a man to help himself, but do not expend all your efforts in helping a man who will not help himself.* [1]

Where do you think Roosevelt would have been as Goliath made his taunts against God? More importantly, where would *you* have been?

---

1. Banks, C. E. and L. Armstrong. *Theodore Roosevelt, Twenty-Sixth President of the United States. A Typical American.* Chicago, 1901.

* * * * *

As leaders in the church, we must be willing to boldly step forward and proclaim the Truth of the Gospel. People are motivated as they hear and understand the Truth of the Scriptures. It is the Word of God that touches hearts.

The purpose of the pastor in the Christian church is to shepherd. The pastor must seek and search out the truths of Scripture and then preach and teach the Word. The Word enters the heart and the Holy Spirit guides us in our path. In order that pastors might fulfill their God given call, we must insure that they are allowed to effectively preach and teach. This takes time, focus and intentionality.

Unfortunately, in too many churches, the pastor's *study* has become the pastor's *office*. Pastors spend much of their time dealing with the tyranny of the urgent issues rather than concentrating on the primary reason for their calling to preach and teach.

While time has always been constant, the distractions of our fast-paced culture have placed increasingly difficult burdens on individuals to manage the allocation of time. Therefore, leaders must consider stewardship not only of finances, but of time as well. If the role of the pastor is to preach and teach, how can the pastoral staff and lay leadership effectively steward the use of time so that the focus of the pastor is not shifted to other matters? (Although David wasn't a "pastor," he was the leader of Israel. What sort of man would he have been if he had neglected his time with God?)

As leaders consider their responsibility to position the church so that God might use it as a tool for His motivation, the issue of time stewardship is crucial. God always gives the church the resources it needs to accomplish His work. The most valuable resource is not a balanced budget. The most valuable resources are the people. It is the responsibility of the leaders to create the environment in which God can best motivate and equip His people so that the entire congregation is engaged in the use of their talents and gifts. This is a church that will glorify God and expand His Kingdom.

If not, we simply sit in our tents . . .

WHO IS THE FOCUS OF OUR MOTIVATION?

Although David is not directly listed as the author of Psalm 121, we can certainly read his personality loudly bursting forth from it. It begins:

> *I lift up my eyes to the hills—where does my help come from? My help comes from the LORD, the Maker of heaven and earth.*
>
> Psalm 121:1–2

This Psalm is one of the songs of ascent—thought to be part of the traditional liturgy as worshippers ascended to the Temple. The "hills" referred to are most likely Mount Moriah (where the temple was located) and Mount Zion (where the Lord "dwelt"—see Psalm 74). The Psalmist is looking up for the Lord's help.

Therefore, as we seek the summit, leaders must be looking up to the Lord for motivation. David Mains, in his book, *The Sense of His Presence*, clarifies proper focus like this:

> *When the church is functioning at its best, when it is on fire for the Lord, the presence of Christ is the focus of corporate life. In such a church it's not the building of which people are most proud. The pastor isn't the personality whose name dominates all conversations. The denominational program isn't what is pushed most. It is Christ who is the center of interest.*[2]

People will stay properly motivated, as long as the Motivator is consistently before them. We must look up to the Lord, the Maker of heaven and earth. We must consistently remember the love of Christ who died for us. That is our motivation.

I once watched developers build a new subdivision adjacent to my neighborhood. Through it, I learned quite a bit about the building process. They began by clear-cutting all the trees and vegetation in the area. Following that act of destruction, they began leveling off the ground. What was a fascinating project to watch then took an interesting twist—I could no longer see what they are doing! Why not? They began blasting underground in order to lay pipe. A siren blast filled the air and moments later, our walls shook.

Applying this analogy to motivation in your church raises some interesting questions. Do you need to do some clear-cutting of programs? Is it time to level off some "processes" and systems that have gotten out

---

2. Mains, Donald. *Sense of His Presence*. Thomas Nelson Publishing, 1988.

of control? Do you need to do some work "underground"—working in key areas or with key people to set some necessary things in place to effectively move into the future? Are you ready for the church walls to start shaking?

We are no longer our own. We live not for ourselves, but *for Him who died*. Look to the Lord and shake the walls!

Action Steps:

1. In churches, we often find that the leaders know very little about one another. In an effort to bridge the gap of understanding, write your "clarifying moment" in one paragraph. How did He touch your soul with the reality of His existence? How did you come to know the immensity of the gift that He has given to you through His life, death and resurrection? Share these paragraphs with one another at your next leadership meeting.

2. Ask the members of your congregation to write their own one paragraph "clarifying moment." Create a Testimony Journal made up of all the personal moments of your congregation. Make copies of the journal available to members and add new testimonies as new people join your fellowship. (Imagine the size of the book in five years!)

3. Develop a forum to ask your congregation to consider their place in the "Priesthood of Believers" (1st Peter 2:4–10). Help them understand that it is no coincidence that God has brought them to your church. Indicate the willingness of the leadership of the church to help each member discover, develop and deploy their spiritual gifts and talents for the good of the Kingdom.

4. Establish a task force to study the *Tyranny of the Urgent* in your church. Explore how, through team leadership, other church leaders and volunteers might handle some of those "urgent" things that distract the pastor from preaching and teaching. (Implementing this concept in your congregation will probably require some education with firm ground rules. If the reasons are fully communicated and explained, they will be accepted and your church will be blessed.)

3

Obedience

Follow the Boss

In 2007, the movie *Evan Almighty* made a splash on theater screens across the country. Evan was a congressman who ran on the promise to "Change the World." As he steps into a new position of power and influence, God suddenly appears to him and instructs him to build an ark. Although some inevitably quibbled with the theology of the movie, I frankly found it to be a compelling visual of how Noah must have felt when commanded to build the ark.

Have you ever placed yourself in the context of the account of Noah? Let's take a few moments to once again imagine the setting.

> *I am going to put an end to all people, for the earth is filled with violence because of them. I am surely going to destroy both them and the earth. So make yourself an ark of cypress wood . . . But I will establish my covenant with you, and you will enter the ark—you and your sons and your wife and your sons' wives with you. You are to bring into the ark two of all living creatures, male and female to keep them alive with you.*
>
> Genesis 6:13–14a, 18

Because most people were taught this story as infants, it is easy to skim over the details. However, for the purpose of this look at obedience, let's consider the enormity of the command that had been given to Noah.

In the backdrop, we see that all around Noah, people were living their lives—eating, drinking and getting married (Luke 17:27). While this sounds "normal," we see in Genesis 6:5 that *"every inclination of the thoughts of [man's] heart was only evil all the time."*

What an *incredible* pronouncement!

And yet Noah found *favor* in the eyes of the Lord (Genesis 6:8). God determined that this righteous man and his family would live. First though, they had to build an ark . . .

* * * * *

Imagine living next door to Noah. A simple assumption could be that he was going to build a house of some sort. However, you would quickly see that this was a rather unusual structure.

As his neighbor, what would your response be as Noah and his sons labored to build the massive ark and complete the task God set before them? Would you have picked up a hammer to help? I certainly don't think I would have reacted that way.

If I had been Noah's friend, I would have thought about checking him into an institution. When a former neighbor of mine built a fence and, in my opinion, destroyed some beautiful green space, I was about to go through the roof! Again, it is easy to gloss over this fact, but Noah was doing something that was simply crazy!

As we can see, Noah was a different man. His reaction did *not* fit the norm. *Noah did everything just as God commanded him.* (Genesis 6:22) That, my friends, is *obedience*.

* * * * *

So what makes Noah so special? Out of everyone living on the entire earth, how could he be the only person who was considered righteous? Noah had the strength of character to be able to build a huge ark on dry land. *Why* did he do it?

Let's allow the writer of Hebrews to shed some light.

> *By faith Noah, when warned about things not yet seen, in holy fear built an ark to save his family. By his faith he condemned the world and became heir of the righteousness that comes by faith.*
>
> Hebrews 11:7

Noah obeyed because he had faith. It is that simple. Noah had faith enough to obey God and act—even though in the eyes of those around him, he had probably lost his mind. Paul takes the discussion of faith a little deeper when he links obedience and faith together.

> *Through Him and for His name's sake, we received grace and apostleship to call people from among all the Gentiles to the obedience that comes from faith. And you also are among those who are called to belong to Jesus Christ.*
>
> Romans 1:5–6

Obedience comes from faith. God's grace is bestowed upon us so that we are able to call non-believers to the obedience that originates from faith. Our faith is in Christ and we follow Him. As we follow, we become obedient. Then, as Christ's followers, we are "mirrors" of Him that reflect His light (2nd Corinthians 3:18).

Paul also says we belong to Jesus. What does that really mean?

> *Remain in Me and I will remain in you. No branch can bear fruit by itself; it must remain in the vine. Neither can you bear fruit unless you remain in Me. I am the vine; you are the branches. If a man remains in Me and I in him, he will bear much fruit; apart from me you can do nothing. If anyone does not remain in me, he is like a branch that is thrown away and withers; such branches are picked up, thrown into the fire and burned. If you remain in me and my words remain in you, ask whatever you wish, and it will be given you. This is to My Father's glory, that you bear much fruit, showing yourselves to be My disciples. As the Father has loved Me, so I have loved you. Now remain in My love. If you obey My commands, you will remain in My love, just as I have obeyed My Father's commands and remain in His love.*
>
> John 15:4–10

This key passage is crucial when considering the importance of our responsibility in church effectiveness. We obey God out of faith. Our faith is then strengthened as we remain close to God, live in obedience to His Word and see His faithfulness. If we stray from God, our faith will be weakened. We must stay connected by abiding in Him. We will be very effective for the Kingdom. The message is very simple.

> *But the one who hears my words and does not put them into practice is like a man who built a house on the ground without a foundation. The moment the torrent struck the house, it collapsed and its destruction was complete.*
>
> Luke 6:49

Our effectiveness must be built on the firm foundation of our faith in and obedience to Jesus Christ. Obedience follows faith. Effectiveness follows obedience.

Is Noah offering you a hammer?

GUIDING PRINCIPLE

True knowledge of God is born out of obedience.
—John Calvin

THE CHALLENGE OF LEADERSHIP

On the first day of school, teachers review the classroom rules. They instruct the children on how they are to behave. As the days progress, the students are reminded of the classroom rules so that they know them without being reminded. Simply put, they are expected to obey the rules because there are rules.

Calvin's quote above is interesting in its approach. The more we seek to be obedient, the more knowledgeable of God we will become. This flies in the face of normal human logic which would say that the more we learn about God, the more we will be willing to be obedient.

As we wrestle with this concept, the key is to understand the concept of God's mercy and grace. As He opens our eyes to the Truth and richness of His grace, we then *desire* to respond in loving appreciation. This spurs us to obedience. This obedience is motivated not out of fear, but out of love. As we obey and follow God, our knowledge of His love deepens. Obedience in the Christian walk involves practicing spiritual disciplines.

An appropriately obedient response has many dimensions that impact leaders. Therefore, leaders in the church need to understand the component of obedience in light of two principles:

1. Leaders must help people to understand that as Christians, we have been called to live lives very different from the world.
2. Christians must understand what it means to live an obedient life in Christ.

In addressing those two principles, we must ask the following questions:

- What does it mean to be obedient to the calling of Christ?
- How can we best assure our obedience to Christ?
- How will we abide in Jesus Christ?
- How can we best position ourselves to be used for His best purposes?

Moving through a discussion of these questions and then working through the exercises will help both you and the other leaders in your church to explore the power of obedience born of faith. We will explore Noah's life as a model of this component of effective churches.

WHAT DOES IT MEAN TO BE OBEDIENT TO THE CALLING OF CHRIST?

I still remember the first time my son didn't respond to "Because daddy said so." It started out simply enough. We were cleaning up at the end of the day and I told him to help with a certain task. His question of "Why, daddy?" didn't surprise me. Questions are par for the course with young children. (I once read a statistic that stated children ask an average of 439 questions each day!) Being a semi-normal father, I gave the standard answer of "Because I said so." He very politely replied, "Yes daddy, but why?"

Have you ever asked God, "Yes Daddy, but why?" I must confess I have on several occasions. Scripture does not record this question from Noah. Instead, it states rather simply:

> *Noah did everything just as God commanded him.*
> Genesis 6:22

Noah was a special man to be able to follow God's seemingly outrageous instruction. As I talk with believers and those not in the family of faith, some would also consider obedience through the practice of spiritual disciples to be likewise. But faith calls us to do some things that are rather unusual in the eyes of the world.

Faith in Jesus causes us to respond with *loving appreciation*. True obedience is a natural outgrowth of Godly motivation. Obedience is a function of true faith. If we have even an elementary understanding of the extent of His love for us and in turn we seek to respond to Him in love, we will have an inbred desire to be obedient to His calling on our lives.

It is so crucial to understand that the components of the effective church are built systematically upon a solid foundation. The foundation of all things must be the Word. In Scripture, Christ tells us that we have a command to love one another (John 13:34–35). Therefore, one of the essential elements in our foundation is love.

Thinking back to my son, he trusted me enough to know that I loved him and had his best interests at heart. Noah knew that God hated the evil in the world and yet loved His creation enough to sustain it through the purging of evil.

As parents build a foundation of love in the home, the foundation of love must be laid in the church. This foundation spurs the response of motivation that is filled with loving appreciation. Upon this, obedience develops. John Mac Arthur once said:

> *To understand and to affirmatively respond to the truth of the Gospel of Jesus Christ is to have one's time and eternity completely altered.*

It really is exciting to think about this calling to obedience. After being called by God to follow Him, you passionately want to respond out of sheer appreciation. That response of appreciation drives you to determine exactly what course He has planned for you. Scripture states it plainly.

> *I know, O Lord, that a man's life is not his own; it is not for man to direct his steps.*
>
> Jeremiah 10:23

> *In his heart a man plans his course, but the LORD determines his steps.*
>
> Proverbs 16:9

So what does it mean to be an obedient leader in the church? Or rather, how does obedience manifest itself in leadership? The New Testament supplies us with a thorough list of leadership criteria. Understanding this list helps us to discern the first reality of leadership criteria. The Scriptural qualifications Paul presents through the Holy Spirit in 1st Timothy and Titus 1 are these:

> We are to be:
>
> Blameless, hospitable, lovers of goodness, self-controlled, upright, holy, self-disciplined, holding to the Word as taught, able to give instruction in sound doctrine, able to refute those who would oppose doctrine, above reproach, with good reputation, respectable, able to teach, gentle, good managers of our households, raisers of believing children, sincere, tested first, faithful, full of the Spirit and wise.
>
> We are not to be:
>
> Overbearing, quick-tempered, violent, greedy for gain, quarrelsome, lovers of money, recent converts or addicted to much wine.

To put it simply, these lists are humbling. Bill Hull, in his book, *Building High Commitment in a Low Commitment World*, boldly summarizes the criteria appointing church leadership: "*An obedient church is one that appoints leaders who are gifted and spiritually suited for the task—anything less is sin.*"

A Godly leader understands that, based on one's own qualifications, he or she is totally unworthy to serve as God's instrument. Therefore, they must be constantly seeking His power, wisdom and strength in order to be effective. He is the potter and we are the clay.

HOW CAN WE BEST ASSURE OUR OBEDIENCE TO CHRIST?

Midway through chapter nine of Genesis, we are able to read an interesting account involving Noah and his three sons.

> *Noah, a man of the soil, proceeded to plant a vineyard. When he drank some of its wine, he became drunk and lay uncovered inside*

> *his tent. Ham, the father of Canaan, saw his father's nakedness and told his two brothers outside. But Shem and Japheth took a garment and laid it across their shoulders; then they walked in backward and covered their father's nakedness. Their faces were turned the other way so that they would not see their father's nakedness.*

Gen 9:20–23

Noah, our example of obedience, was a farmer. Because part of this account is told with the fast-forward button pressed, we see that he was a successful farmer. The vineyard produces grapes which he made into wine. He drank too much and passed out. Ham saw this and proceeded to tell his brothers.

Think about that for a minute. Imagine the moment of Ham leaving his father. I find it difficult to not interpose my own perceptions of the situation. If I'm stretching too far, I'll have to just ask your forgiveness.

Noah was an incredible success. His sons were witnesses of his obedience in following God's direction. They entered the ark with their father and watched as the world was destroyed. They rode out the waves with him and watched as the waters receded. They left the ark together. They watched as he built an altar to the Lord and received God' blessing. They saw him plant a vineyard that produced a harvest.

That's a pretty tough role model to live up to…

Sons watch their fathers. When fathers are highly successful, there is pressure on the sons to follow that same path. Again, I may be stretching my reading of the passage, but I think the actions of Ham reflect that he may have gone outside to tell his brothers that their father was human after all. The "perfect" Noah had passed out and was now laying exposed.

However, Shem and Japheth—rather than reveling in the situation—acted honorably. They walked backwards into the tent and covered their father.

I wonder how Ham *then* felt about his actions and the actions of his brothers?

And this brings us back to our question of assuring our obedience to Christ. Let's look at the book of Hebrews for an answer.

> *Therefore, holy brothers, who share in the heavenly calling, fix your thoughts on Jesus, the apostle and high priest in whom we confess.*

Hebrews 3:1

Noah fixed his thoughts on obedience to God. He followed the Lord's directions and sought to live out His will in life. The new covenant calls for us to fix our thoughts on Jesus and seek to live out our faith in Him.

The first thing this requires is confession and repentance. This message has been trumpeted since the fall of man in the Garden. God will not use us if we are not able to first acknowledge our sinfulness, realize our inadequacies and lean on Him for our empowerment. Only the repentant heart can be used by God.

> *For the grace of God that brings salvation has appeared to all men. It teaches us to say "No" to ungodliness, worldly passions, and to live self-controlled, upright and godly lives in this present age, while we wait for the blessed hope—the glorious appearing of our great God and Savior, Jesus Christ, who gave Himself for us to redeem us from all wickedness and to purify for Himself a people that are His very own, eager to do what is good.*
>
> Titus 2:11–14

Obedience to Christ can only be assured through submission to Christ. We need to surround ourselves with His teaching. Think for a moment of a swimming pool. Can you swim if you never get in the water? Dipping your toes into the edge is never going to get you wet.

In the walk of Christian faith, we must jump in and totally immerse ourselves in the waters of Christ. It is this depth of abiding in Him that guides our course and helps us to be leaders at home, at work and in the church.

And this leads us to the next application of abiding in Christ.

HOW WILL WE ABIDE IN JESUS CHRIST?

Before we can answer the question of how a believer will abide in Christ, we must first agree on the definition of the word "abide." Although the word can have various nuances, the working definition used here is that which means to stand fast, remain stable or dwell within something or someone.

Scripturally, the illustration of abiding in Christ is found in John 15 (cited earlier in the introduction of this chapter). This is often called the *Parable of the Vine*.

> *Remain in me, and I will remain in you. No branch can bear fruit by itself; it must remain in the vine. Neither can you bear fruit unless you remain in me. "I am the vine; you are the branches. If a man remains in me and I in him, he will bear much fruit; apart from me you can do nothing.*
>
> John 15:4-5

It should be obvious that it is impossible for a branch to live apart from the vine. From the vine, sustenance is received. Water, nutrients, etc. ... come through this connection. The branch is also a part of something bigger than the branch itself. Without the rest of the plant, the branch is only a dried out stick.

Therefore, as we seek to understand this in application to the Christian life, we must understand what God requires of us. How are we a part of the Kingdom? What specifically is Christ calling us to do as we respond to him? We are saved by grace, but what is our responsibility beyond accepting our salvation? What are God's intentions for us? This question has been a wrestling point for both theologians and lay people. The theologians of the seventeenth century approached this question and responded to it through the Westminster Confession of Faith.

The third question of the Shorter Catechism and its answer are as follows:

> Question 3: What do the Scriptures principally teach? The Scriptures principally teach, what man is to believe concerning God, and what duty God requires of man.

The Reformers recognized that God's gift of grace to us was not to stand in isolation. There must be some spiritual response from us. Just how are we to determine the appropriate level of response?

We must first understand that our obedience cannot be based on our attempt in any way to repay Christ based on what He has done for us. Human obedience is fully unsatisfactory. There is no amount of sacrifice or devotion that even approaches sufficiency when we consider the enormity of what God has done for us. Mankind cannot repay God for His gift of redemption through Jesus Christ.

Does this mean that we then succumb to our ineptitude, rationalizing that there is nothing that we can do to pay Him back? Therefore, any effort on our part is meaningless and there is no use in committing any part of our lives to Him? That is obviously irrational thinking also.

Consider the early church and the disciples that were closest to Jesus Christ physically and spiritually. These were the men that knew Him best. We must consider their willingness to commit their lives to Him. Nearly all of those early followers literally gave their lives for Him. Their obedience was inspired. Their obedience was total. Consider this example from Paul:

> *Are they servants of Christ? (I am out of my mind to talk like this.) I am more. I have worked much harder, been in prison more frequently, been flogged more severely, and been exposed to death again and again. Five times I received from the Jews the forty lashes minus one. Three times I was beaten with rods, once I was stoned, three times I was shipwrecked, I spent a night and a day in the open sea, I have been constantly on the move. I have been in danger from rivers, in danger from bandits, in danger from my own countrymen, in danger from Gentiles; in danger in the city, in danger in the country, in danger at sea; and in danger from false brothers. I have labored and toiled and have often gone without sleep; I have known hunger and thirst and have often gone without food; I have been cold and naked. Besides everything else, I face daily the pressures of my concern for all the churches.*
>
> 2 Corinthians 11:23–28

Is this the kind of sacrifice and suffering that Christ expects of us today? Can any of us say that we have experienced even a small amount of persecution equivalent to that which Paul endured for the sake of the cross? How then can we know what obedience means for us?

As we abide in Christ, we "stay attached" to God so that He can continue to work on us and through us. There is an implication of consistency and perseverance in the concept of abiding in Christ. It implies that we must seek ways to assure an ongoing connection with Him. There must be a constant attachment so that we can continue to draw strength from the Source.

As you continue to reflect on what it means to abide in Christ, the following principles can be considered as a way to enhance your spiritual walk. They will help us to abide in Christ. This path of obedience has served as a formula for followers of Christ throughout the centuries.

PRINCIPLE ONE:

> *In order to position ourselves so that we are ready, willing and able to accomplish God's plan for our lives, we must be seeking to become more Christ-like. The more obedient we are to God's calling to godliness, the more effective we will be in His use.*

Effective church leaders are in constant touch with God. How can we expect our ministry through our churches to be blessed and impactful, if we do not have a vibrant, consistent relationship with God? To understand this in detail, we move to Principle number two.

PRINCIPLE TWO:

> *The most straightforward path to godliness is to understand the spiritual disciplines and to consistently live a more spiritually disciplined life.*

If there is to be any "striving" in our quest to be more obedient either as Christians or as Christian leaders, our striving should be *towards godliness*, not towards being better Christians or better Christian leaders. There is a difference.

This quest toward Christ-likeness can be accomplished as we seek to be more disciplined Christians. Donald Whitney describes spiritual discipline as follows in his book, *Spiritual Disciplines for the Christian Life*:

> *The Spiritual Disciplines are those personal and corporate disciplines that promote spiritual growth. They are the habits of devotion and experiential Christianity that have been practiced by the people of God since Biblical times. The Spiritual Disciplines are the God-given means we are to use in the Spirit-filled pursuit of Godliness.*[1]

The Spiritual Disciplines as described in Whitney's list are as follows:

- Bible intake:
    - Hearing the Word
    - Reading the Word
    - Memorizing the Word
    - Meditating on the Word

---

1. Whitney, Donald. *Spiritual Disciplines for the Christian Life*. NavPress Publishing Group, 1997.

- Prayer
- Worship
- Evangelism
- Serving
- Stewardship
- Fasting
- Silence and Solitude
- Learning
- Journaling

It is no coincidence that this list includes most of the things to which the 1st Century church devoted itself. To modern, busy Christians, a list this all-encompassing can be overwhelming. In this century, the pace of life is much more frantic. How can we be expected to spend more time becoming more spiritually disciplined? If we devote ourselves to spending more time to become more spiritually mature, He will multiple our time. This is a spiritual phenomenon that is logically incomprehensible but practically true.

PRINCIPLE THREE:

Spiritual Discipline in the pursuit of Godliness is accomplishable! God would not call us to endeavors that are beyond our scope of doing. (But we must rely on His help.)

We don't need to understand this principle. We just need to believe it. As Christians—and more importantly, as Christian *leaders*—our first and foremost responsibility is to seek to be more Christ-like. As we make time to grow closer to Him, He will give us the time to accomplish the things that are important to Him. We must take steps toward our growth. We do not grow in every discipline at once, but He will call us to focus on specific disciplines at specific times in our lives.

The visual picture of Noah and his family "abiding" in God is wonderful. Not only did they obey God's commandment to build an ark, they entered it and God shut the door (Genesis 7:16). They listened to the rain for 40 nights, *trusting in God's promises.*

The earth was flooded for 150 days—and *they trusted in God's promises.*

They watched as the waters receded from the earth and the tops of the mountains became visible—and *they trusted in God's promises.*

For forty days, Noah sent out a raven—and *they trusted in God's promises.*

Three times, Noah sent out a dove—and *they trusted in God's promises.*

Noah and his family personified "abiding" in God. They stood fast and trusted.

HOW CAN WE POSITION OURSELVES TO BE BEST USED FOR HIS PURPOSES?

The first thing Noah and his family did upon leaving the ark was to glorify God. They built an altar and offered sacrifices on it. And God responded by making a covenant with Noah and his family that the earth would never be flooded again.

> *And God said, "This is the sign of the covenant I am making between me and you and every living creature with you, a covenant for all generations to come: I have set my rainbow in the clouds, and it will be the sign of the covenant between me and the earth.*
>
> Genesis 9:12–13

In abiding with God, Noah was in a position to be used as His instrument. As we seek to abide in Christ, we need to open ourselves to be used by God. He will use us as instruments of His kingdom. In His sovereignty, God will position us to be used as He directs our path. This is one of the remarkable and hard to believe truths of our faith. Our responsibility is not the "work of the church." *Our responsibility is to walk in a manner worthy of His calling.* As we seek Him and grow in Him, we are positioned for His use. Spiritual discipline molds us and sculpts us into effective vessels.

The simple truth is that the great leaders of Christendom never strove to be great Christian leaders. They were devoted to growing closer to God. God then used them as great leaders because they had positioned themselves for His greatest use. They were plugged into His power. Billy Graham was once asked, "If you had to live your life over again, what would you do differently?" His response?

> *One of my great regrets is that I have not studied enough. I wish I had studied more and preached less. People have pressured me into*

> *speaking to groups when I should have been studying and preparing. Donald Barnhouse said that if he knew the Lord was coming in three years, he would spend two of them studying and one preaching. (As quoted in Christianity Today, September 12, 1977)*

This is not "normal" to the world. As Paul admonishes us:

> *Therefore, I urge you, brothers, in view of God's mercy, to offer your bodies as living sacrifices, holy and pleasing to God—this is your spiritual act of worship. Do not conform any longer to the pattern of this world, but be transformed by the renewing of your mind. Then you will be able to test and approve what God's will is—His good, pleasing and perfect will.*
>
> Romans 12:1–2

This passage summarizes the essence of spiritual obedience.

- We are to offer our bodies obediently to God as living sacrifices.
- We are not to conform to the pattern of this world.
- We are to be transformed by the renewing of our minds.
- Then we will be able to know God's will for us.

In effective churches, people are obedient to God's calling. They understand that in order to be used by God, they must continually be mindful that He is the source of true power and effectiveness. They know that to take advantage of that power they must stay attached to the vine.

> *If you remain in me and my words remain in you, ask whatever you wish, and it will be given to you.*
>
> John 15:7

Action Steps:

1. Growth is vital in our walk with the Lord.
   a. Take some time to do a personal spiritual inventory of your walk with the Lord over the last 12 months. In which areas of your life have you grown in your obedience to the Lord? In which of the areas of spiritual discipline do you feel the most comfortable?

   _____
   _____
   _____
   _____
   _____
   _____

   b. Again, considering the list of spiritual disciplines, in which areas do you believe you need more work? How is God prompting you right now to commit more intentionally to one or more of these disciplines?

   _____
   _____
   _____
   _____
   _____
   _____

2. Schedule some time in both your leadership meetings and as a church to conduct some specific teaching and perhaps a pulpit series on repentance and God's grace. Plan a special service devoted to nothing but repentance, praise and worship for God's mercy. Offer a time for individuals to repent of their individual sinfulness and for congregational sins of omission and commission. This type of cleansing and celebration will be both pleasing to God and refreshing to the Body of Believers.

3. Form small groups to study the topic of Spiritual Disciplines. Donald Whitney's book, *Spiritual Disciplines for the Christian Faith*, is an excellent basis for this course. (Companion study guide is available. Contact LRM for quantity discounts.)

4. Encourage your leadership and small groups to consider accountability as a major dynamic of their existence. We all need someone to hold us accountable and the depth of relationship and intimacy in small groups provides a perfect forum for healthy Christian accountability. As we encourage and challenge one another in our Christian walk, we will all grow closer to God.

4

Attitude

The Right Face

In 2008, Tim Gannon, the founder of Outback Steakhouse, was asked in an interview with USA Today a question relating to first jobs for teens[1]. He replied that he had yet to meet a successful person who didn't have a great story about starting on the ground floor. *"Great success comes from overcoming adversity. Without desire, you can't get to ambition."*

Having worked with (and for) a number of less than stellar employees (and been one myself on occasion), I know how important attitude is on the job. It makes a great difference as we are seeking to fulfill our responsibilities. There are two sides to attitude: the giving and the receiving.

In giving, or perhaps we should say "projecting," the right attitude, we must consider our responsibility to be a reflection of Christ (2nd Corinthians 3:18). As we go about our work, be it at home, in the office or at church, people should see sincerity in who we are and what we are doing.

In receiving the right attitude, we should be open to seeing Christ in others. As we all know and have experienced, not everyone will have the right motivations behind them. However, that does not mean we should limit ourselves by having a negative approach. We need to speak positively towards others and encourage the right attitude from them.

As brothers and sisters in Christ, we recognize that we are actually the chosen co-heirs of the Kingdom of God. Our attitudes and the way we live our lives should present to others that we are eternally influenced.

---

1. CEOs value lessons from teen jobs; by Del Jones; June 5, 2008; USA Today, a division of Gannett Co., Inc.

Scripture is very clear about the appropriate state of mind for those under the influence of the Holy Spirit.

> *But the fruit of the Spirit is love, joy, peace, patience, kindness, goodness, faithfulness, gentleness and self-control. Against such things there is no law.*
>
> Galatians 5:22–23

Our attitudes both in church and out of church should reflect God's call on our lives to live as if we are God's and to relate to one another differently as brothers and sisters in Christ. Isolationists are not allowed in church! We are called to support and encourage one another. The walk of a Christian is a journey as part of a joy-filled community.

> *Rejoice in the Lord always. I will say it again: Rejoice! Let your gentleness be evident to all. The Lord is near.*
>
> Philippians 4:4–5

The Lord will support us in our attitude of joy. As we stay close to Him, our joy will be complete.

> *To Him who is able to keep you from falling and to present you before His glorious presence without fault and with great joy—to the only God our Savior be glory, majesty, power and authority, through Jesus Christ our Lord, before all ages, now and forevermore! Amen.*
>
> Jude 1:24–25

In the end, it is God that provides us with the attitude that is pleasing to Him, as we surrender our will to Him. It is a process of daily surrender and release. If we simply let His radiance be reflected through us, our countenance will be pleasing to Him. As a result, it will make a difference to those around us as well—both those we are serving with and those whom we are serving.

In our exploration of the 4th component in the tier of Mission, we are going to use Joseph, the 11th son of Jacob as our example. As we learn in Genesis chapters 37–50, he was a man whom God began using from a very early age. The dreams he was given set forward a bold path and audacious purpose for his life.

However, it was Joseph's projection of himself and the reception of his dreams by others that directed his path down a difficult road . . .

* * * * *

We're going to kill you. No, come to think of it, if we did that, you would just be dead. How about if we just sell you into slavery. That way, we'll get some money and you will suffer before you eventually die.

Hard to imagine, isn't it?

Joseph is an incredibly intriguing character in Scripture. Charting the roller coaster of highs and lows in his life is a guaranteed way of helping a person think that maybe his or her own life isn't so bad after all!

Let's quickly review his life.

His self-important attitude and preferential treatment had frustrated his brothers to the point of not speaking to him.

> *When his brothers saw that their father loved him more than any of them, they hated him and could not speak to him.*
>
> Genesis 37:4

They finally decided to act after his second dream.

> *"Here comes that dreamer!" they said to each other. "Come now, let's kill him and throw him into one of these cisterns and say that a ferocious animal devoured him. Then we'll see what comes of his dreams."*
>
> Genesis 37:19–20

Deciding that wouldn't be proper or profitable, they then decided to sell him into slavery. Jumping ahead in his life, Joseph was actually blessed in his time of slavery so that he was promoted to the second in command. His master's wife attempted to seduce him, but he stayed true to God and his earthly master. She lies to get revenge and Joseph gets thrown into jail. Again, God blesses him so that the prison warden put Joseph in charge of all that was done in the prison.

> *The warden paid no attention to anything under Joseph's care, because the LORD was with Joseph and gave him success in whatever he did.*
>
> Genesis 39:23

In prison, he interprets two dreams for a baker and a cupbearer, but is quickly forgotten when the cupbearer was released from prison. (Personally, I would have been tempted to give up at that point if I had been Joseph, but God is faithful to him.) The cupbearer points Pharaoh to Joseph to interpret a dream and Joseph becomes number two in the entire kingdom of Egypt.

Several years later, the opportunity for revenge presents itself. His family comes to Egypt to get food during the famine and Joseph has the opportunity to punish his brothers for the suffering they caused him. What does he do instead? He takes care of everyone and provides them with more than they could have imagined. In one of the most powerful passages of forgiveness in Scripture, he tells his brothers after the death of his father, Jacob:

> *Don't be afraid. Am I in the place of God? You intended to harm me, but God intended it for good to accomplish what is now being done, the saving of many lives.*
>
> Genesis 50:19–20

God first, self second. Every time I read that passage, I am amazed at the true enormity of that statement. A death threat, slavery, jail, forgotten about and then he comes back with "Hey, it's ok! God had a plan!" Would you have had the same attitude?

GUIDING PRINCIPLE

I believe the single most significant decision I can make on a day-to-day basis is my choice of attitude. Attitude is that one thing that keeps me going or cripples my progress. It alone fuels my fire or assaults my hope.

—Charles Swindoll

THE CHALLENGE OF LEADERSHIP

If leaders are not outwardly energized and enthusiastic by what God is presently doing and what He *could* be doing through the church, there is little chance that the membership will want to be involved in the work of the church.

Attitude is the catalyst that generates action. Sports teams spend hours upon hours building up team morale and motivation to defeat the upcoming opposition. Teams often put gag orders on players to prevent them from saying anything that might be used as fuel to spark the energy of their foes. The right "speech" given by the coach at half-time can propel a team to victory or allow it to slide into defeat. Victory is the only option.

As God's chosen leaders in the church, you are the coaches to rally your team to effectiveness. Your attitudes will be reflected in the faces of your followers. If you are not excited, why would you expect anyone else to be?

We will look at five key questions while addressing the component of attitude. It is important that leaders understand this component before we proceed to our first checkpoint and switchback.

- Why is *attitude* a crucial part of the mission of the church?
- How is the attitude in highly effective churches different?
- What is the frame of mind of Christ-like leaders in the successful church?
- How do we "take-on" the appropriate leadership attitude?
- How much difference does attitude make as we chart the future course of our church?

WHY IS ATTITUDE A CRUCIAL PART OF THE MISSION OF THE CHURCH TODAY?

Joseph is a humbling figure to the receptive heart. How can we look at his life, what he endured and then have the audacity to complain? A God-focused attitude is an incredible thing to observe. A life witnessing God's hand and faithfulness enabled Joseph to say to his brothers:

> "Don't be afraid. Am I in the place of God? You intended to harm me, but God intended it for good to accomplish what is now being

> *done, the saving of many lives. So then, don't be afraid. I will provide for you and your children." And he reassured them and spoke kindly to them.*

Genesis 50:19–21

Let's take a moment to consider the backdrop of these verses. In Genesis, Joseph had a dream that he shared with his brothers.

> *He said to them, "Listen to this dream I had: We were binding sheaves of grain out in the field when suddenly my sheaf rose and stood upright, while your sheaves gathered around mine and bowed down to it."*

Genesis 37:6–7

This prophetic dream was not received well by his brothers. Why not? Let's back up even further...

His father Jacob had fallen *passionately* in love with a beautiful woman named Rachel. So deep was his love for her, that he subjected himself to servitude for seven years to his uncle Laban. Then, when Laban tricked him at the end of seven years, Jacob was willing to serve another seven for his love. It was not easy work but to Jacob, it seemed as if no time had passed (see Genesis 29:20). After he had worked these fourteen years, he agreed to work even longer in order to have some livestock that he could use to begin their lives as a family.

At the end of twenty years, Jacob noticed that Laban's *attitude* had turned against him. Literally, the Hebrew word for "face" is used in the passage. Jacob could tell from the countenance of Laban that he was no longer welcome. This prompts Jacob to speak with his wives and they agree to leave. Laban chases him and they have a confrontation. Jacob finally has an outburst.

> *"I have been with you for twenty years now. Your sheep and goats have not miscarried, nor have I eaten rams from your flocks. I did not bring you animals torn by wild beasts; I bore the loss myself. And you demanded payment from me for whatever was stolen by day or night. This was my situation: The heat consumed me in the daytime and the cold at night, and sleep fled from my eyes. It was like this for the twenty years I was in your household. I worked for you fourteen years for your two daughters and six years for your flocks, and you changed my wages ten times."*

Genesis 31:38–41

Jacob and Laban then part company (Genesis 31:51–53), putting down boundary markers and agreeing never to see one another again. On Jacob's way to see his father, Isaac, Rachel gives birth to Benjamin and dies in the process.

* * * * *

This important context surrounds Joseph's life. While he was not the last son born to Jacob, he was his favorite. He was the firstborn of Rachel—the one whom Jacob had served Laban for fourteen years to "earn." Benjamin, while being the last son of Jacob, would have been a reminder of the death of Rachel.

Joseph was spoiled.

Joseph was the eleventh son of Jacob. He should have been the eleventh in line for an inheritance. But Joseph was the first son of Jacob's true love, Rachel. He was the one who reminded Jacob of her and was truly his pride.

Commentators have debated Joseph's pride for years. Many speculate that Joseph had an attitude of privilege and did not hesitate to remind his brothers of his status as the "favorite." The fact that Joseph was so quick to share his dream with his brothers (and later, another dream with his father) gives great credence to this idea.

But, years later, Joseph has a different attitude. His words at the end of Genesis prove that God had changed his heart dramatically. Rather than being spoiled, bitter and angry, Joseph was kind, forgiving and loving. He continued to care for his brothers when there was no reason to be. God used Joseph's trials to teach him an attitude whereby he would submit himself to God's perfect plan for his life.

Rather than take vengeance, Joseph took on an attitude of love and service.

* * * * *

Why are we spending so much time reflecting on Joseph?

Attitude is the third checkpoint in our journey of effective leadership development. This component completes the underlying level of mission. These components are part of a bigger picture. They are a mind-set. They are a philosophy of ministry. They are the model of the environment that will help you to "do church" the way God intended it to be done. If fully understood and in place for the church to flourish, the work of the church *will* be more effectively accomplished.

As the last foundational checkpoint, attitude is the thrust of power to the previous components. Motivation flowing from loving appreciation for God's mercy inspires us to service. As God motivates the church, it becomes more obedient to Him. Obedience grows from motivation as the spiritual disciplines deepen and mature our faith. An expectant, high-energy attitude is the resulting outpouring of God's providence within the congregation.

Attitude is everything is a saying fully applicable in the life of the church. Human beings require encouragement and stimulation on a day-to-day basis. We want our endeavors to be extremely significant and highly effective. Time is too valuable to waste on what we perceive to be ineffective or futile exercises.

For maximum impact, attitude must be genuine. We don't have to drum up artificial excitement about the importance of a God-given mission because there is no more important endeavor. We are doing God's work. We are His instruments for a lost and dying world. What could be more important? This attitudinal mind set needs to be activated, reinforced and continually nurtured. A high level of spiritual energy in the church will be self-fulfilling. We are God's work force. That is exciting!

HOW IS THE ATTITUDE IN HIGHLY EFFECTIVE CHURCHES DIFFERENT?

Joseph's attitude was exemplified through the kindness and love demonstrated to his brothers. As we look at another example from his life, we can see a point at which he could have completely given up on God and most people would not have thought anything negative about him.

Joseph's brothers had sold him into slavery and falsified evidence of his death. The Ishmaelites took him far away from his family and his life was in their hands—or so they assumed.

> *Now Joseph had been taken down to Egypt. Potiphar, an Egyptian who was one of Pharaoh's officials, the captain of the guard, bought him from the Ishmaelites who had taken him there.*
>
> Genesis 39:1

Joseph, having lived life as the favored son, was now a slave. However, instead of rebelling, Joseph accepted this position and worked hard. God blessed his work and gave him success. In fact, God blessed Joseph so much that he became the second to only Potiphar himself. Then, because he was young, strong, and handsome, Potiphar's wife attempted to seduce him. Joseph resisted. Rather than being blessed again for doing the right thing, he was thrown into prison.

It's at this point that I think I would have given up. If I hadn't given up, I certainly would have been asking God the *"Why me?"* questions.

But Joseph continued to serve God. And God blessed him.

> *But while Joseph was there in the prison, the LORD was with him; he showed him kindness and granted him favor in the eyes of the prison warden. So the warden put Joseph in charge of all those held in the prison, and he was made responsible for all that was done there. The warden paid no attention to anything under Joseph's care, because the LORD was with Joseph and gave him success in whatever he did.*

Genesis 39:20–23

Joseph kept up an attitude of submission to God's will and lordship in his life. As we will discuss with our next question, there is a specific frame of mind of Christ-like leaders in effective churches. But first, we need to reflect on the overall attitude of effective churches.

In the years that I have served as part of the team at Lay Renewal Ministries, I have visited a *great* number of churches. Without naming names, let's consider two examples:

CHURCH A

As I studied their survey data and reflected on the pastor's information, the one word that came to me that described their attitude was "introverted." It had been months since a visitor had entered. The youth and children's ministries were non-existent. The building was aging rapidly. The budget was in decline.

When I visited the church, I checked three doors before I found one that would open. As I met people, instead of smiles, I was met with wary looks. Each question I asked to gather more information was met with defensiveness or outright hostility.

Bottom-line? I didn't want to stick around and I was being paid to be there!

CHURCH B

Usually I know very clearly why I am going to a church. I've studied the information about the church and community. I've tracked data and prayed. I've had that "one thing" placed on my heart that I hope to see come to fruition. And yet, even though I'd done all of this, I didn't know what I could offer this particular church.

When I left, I knew what the church had given me. Yes, I had still facilitated the event and worked through the materials, but I was truly the one who was blessed. The difference with this church was a completely different attitude.

I was welcomed mightily. There was an intense passion for God. There was an intense passion for the community. This church—while not being incredibly large or wealthy—was filled with people who simply and clearly loved the Lord. That love was poured out like a flood!

Bottom-line? If I didn't have a family waiting for me back home, I might have considered staying!

There is something special that moves in churches that have an intensity for the Gospel. Of course, this "something" is the Holy Spirit. The outward manifestation of His work is projected through the attitudes of the church members. Ministry grows, outreach is enhanced, spiritual growth is sought after and even finances are strong.

Think of it in context of parenting. What does a parent do when their child brings home an indiscernible painting from preschool? What does a parent do when their child receives a positive grade on a school project on which they have labored? What happens when a child makes the team or receives a role in a school play? When a child does their best on a test, what should a parent do? *CHEER!* It is the responsibility of every parent to encourage their children and praise them when they have accomplished a goal or done their best.

Leaders in successful churches are intentional cheerleaders. Their goal is to encourage and to build up the Body at every opportunity. For this enthusiasm to be genuine, leaders need to believe in God's vision for the church themselves. When considering the spiritual attributes of *future* leaders, attitude should be a major consideration. Do not start to build your house with those who will only tear it down through a negative attitude!

WHAT IS THE FRAME OF MIND OF CHRIST-LIKE LEADERS IN SUCCESSFUL CHURCHES?

When he was cast into prison, Joseph was put in charge of other prisoners. In chapter 40, we see that two men, a cupbearer and a baker were thrown into jail for offending Pharaoh. These men were assigned to Joseph and they remained in his care for some time.

Let's slow down and consider a few things. Joseph had freedom to travel about and care for other prisoners. In fact, he was given charge of caring for two men who could potentially have had powerful voices if Pharaoh changed his mind about them. (As we later see, Pharaoh had a little birthday party and restored the cupbearer to his former position.)

What I'd like us to focus on though, is the attitude that exists behind verse seven.

> *So he asked Pharaoh's officials who were in custody with him in his master's house, "Why are your faces so sad today?"*
>
> Genesis 40:7

In inquiring about the expressions on their faces, Joseph wasn't just taking care of their physical needs. He was concerned for their emotional needs as well. He genuinely wanted to know why they were upset. True leaders care for the people.

Successful churches embrace attitudes worthy of an all-powerful God who has entrusted them with His perfect plan. Remember, success is not measured by the world's standards of numeric and financial prowess. Rather, in the church it is measured by the conformity of a church to the plan of God. The dimensions of a Christ-like attitude that encourage success therefore include:

- Energy
- Excitement
- Excellence
- Enthusiasm

- Encouragement
- Expectation
- Empowerment

When God gives us our vision—and we know it is truly from God—there is *energy*. We embrace the reality that we have been given an assignment from the Almighty God who assures us that we cannot fail as we progress in His will.

This energy will stimulate an *excitement* as we seek to serve Him and accomplish His purposes. A God-produced energy will bubble up excitement that will carry throughout the entire congregation.

Because we are serving God, there is only one approach to our ministry. This approach is that all things should be done with *excellence*. All that we do is to give glory to God.

We need to intentionally attack our mission with an *enthusiasm* that is contagious. We are embarking on a journey that will overwhelm us with its success if we hold the course and do our best.

There must be a constant attitude of *encouragement* as we accomplish our mission. An encouraged church filled with excited and enthusiastic people is a tremendous threat to Satan. He will do everything in His power to discourage and wreak havoc on our plan.

We need to reflect a great *expectancy* as to what God is about to do in our presence. A God with no limitations has commissioned us to labor in His service. Only our own timidity and lack of faith will limit our success.

All of this needs to be under-girded with the knowledge that we have the *empowerment* of the Creator of the universe. There is nothing that He cannot accomplish. He has promised to move through us.

HOW DO WE "TAKE-ON" THE APPROPRIATE LEADERSHIP ATTITUDE?

Leadership attitudes will have a monumental impact on the attitudes of the congregation and in turn this will directly affect the success of the church. If only one change is caused because of your exposure to this book, that change needs to be an intentional uplift of your own attitude and that of your leadership team. This change alone will have a tremendous impact on your church.

Attitude: The Right Face

Attitude is a choice. It is that simple. We allow our circumstances to rule us or we rule our circumstances. Consider Joseph. Even though he'd been carried off into slavery and later falsely imprisoned, he still maintained an attitude of God's sovereignty. When the cupbearer and the baker told him they both had dreams and wondered what they meant, Joseph used the opportunity to tell them of God.

After Joseph told the cupbearer the meaning behind his dream, he had one simple request: "Remember me." It wasn't an elaborate request. It wasn't for money, power or fame. Joseph wanted to be freed.

But the cupbearer forgot him for *two full years* (Genesis 41:1).

> God does not forget. God is faithful.

When Pharaoh had dreams that could not be interpreted, the cupbearer remembered Joseph. Pharaoh sent for Joseph and again, when asked to interpret, Joseph gave glory to God.

> *"I cannot do it," Joseph replied to Pharaoh, "but God will give Pharaoh the answer he desires."*
>
> Genesis 41:16

God has mandated attitudinal concepts that we appropriate. We are to "rejoice always." We are to "put on" the full armor of God. We are to "renew our minds." As children of God, we are new beings and our inheritance calls us to respond to life in a new manner. We are to live in a manner worthy of His calling.

One of the dimensions of our Christian walk is joy. James puts it thusly:

> *Consider it pure joy, my brothers, whenever you face trials of many kinds, because you know that the testing of your faith develops perseverance. Perseverance must finish its work so that you may be mature and complete, not lacking anything.*
>
> James 1:2–4

The word "it" is very interesting. What did James mean when he used that simple two-letter word? I would simply argue "it" means "life" or "everything." Consider *life* pure joy whenever trouble comes your way. Not if, but when trouble comes, be joyful. We are to be joyful in all circumstances. We have a choice. We can choose to be joyful or we can choose to not be joyful. However, God tells us which one we should pick.

This is the same phenomenon that we face concerning our attitudes as leaders in the church. We must intentionally take on the dimensions of appropriate attitude as described in the previous section.

HOW MUCH DIFFERENCE DOES ATTITUDE MAKE AS WE CHART THE FUTURE COURSE OF THE CHURCH?

It is really a simple question. As a leader, do you believe that your church has a future? If it does have a future, do you believe it will be a positive one? Ken Callahan states it this way:

> *The watershed question for many people in many congregations is: Do we believe that our best years are behind us, or do we believe that our best years are before us. Either way, it becomes a self-fulfilling prophecy.*[2]

With the interpretation God gave to Joseph, there was also a plan. This plan would provide for the needs of the people of Egypt and the surrounding countries for seven years of famine. Pharaoh recognized that God was with Joseph and wisely put Joseph in a position of incredible power and authority.

> *So Pharaoh asked [his officials], "Can we find anyone like this man, one in whom is the spirit of God?" Then Pharaoh said to Joseph, "Since God has made all this known to you, there is no one so discerning and wise as you. You shall be in charge of my palace, and all my people are to submit to your orders. Only with respect to the throne will I be greater than you."*
>
> Genesis 41:38–40

In his landmark book on business and leadership, *Good to Great*, author Jim Collins pointed out a very important element of leadership teams.

> *Great vision without great people is irrelevant.*[3]

Nothing will tear your team or church apart faster than attitudes of disunity and dissention. Teachers are a great example of this principle. As they prepare for their careers, they taught and re-taught the concept of self-fulfilling prophecy. If a child is presented with the attitude from

---

2. Callahan, Kennon L. *Twelve Keys to an Effective Church.* Jossey-Bass, 1997.
3. Collins, Jim. *Good to Great.* New York: Harper Collins Publishers, Inc., 2001

the parents or teacher that he or she is a failure, the child normally will become that which is expected. Therefore, the teacher's role (in addition to teaching), becomes one in which they must create an atmosphere of success for each and every child.

Similarly, leaders must also convey an attitude and build that atmosphere of success. The vitality and growth of the local church is critically linked to the congregation's attitude about its future. If church leaders can genuinely send the message that *God* has great plans for the future and that nothing can stand in the way of those plans, the congregation will excitedly accept the news and invest their lives and families in that future. Positive momentum grows healthy churches.

It should be obvious that presenting a gloom and doom, imminent disaster characterization of the church's future will only lead others into a like-minded downward spiral of hopelessness. Individuals and families will leave to find somewhere they can invest themselves in a positive future. Negative momentum is as powerful as positive momentum.

In churches that are in trouble, the most significant concerns typically become budget focused. In the successful church, the focus is spiritual and evangelistic.

The challenge to healthy churches is to work hard to sustain the positive momentum. This requires frequently revisiting the dimensions that caused health and prosperity in the first place. We believe that those dimensions are embodied in the components that are being explored in this book. These components are built upon the Word of God.

The challenge for struggling churches is to stop the downward spiral, to refocus on God's Word, God's mission, to rebuild relationships and to do the things necessary to recreate a church that is pleasing to God.

What is the culture that currently controls your church's environment?

Action Steps:

1. Attitude is key to the future of your church. In light of what has been just been discussed, it is appropriate to take a few minutes to do a quick evaluation and examination. What can you personally do to improve your own attitude, that of your leadership team and that of your church? Remember, start with yourself first!
2. Consider the following scale and questions:

    Excited = 5 Hopeful = 4 Ambivalent = 3 Worried = 2 Pessimistic = 1

    a. Personal Attitude Quotient: Based on the above scale, what is your attitude right now about the future of your church?

    b. Leadership Team quotient: In your personal opinion, what is the attitude of your leadership team right now about the future of your church?

    c. Church Attitude Quotient: In your personal opinion, what is the attitude of your congregation right now about the future of the church?

3. Have the leadership team of your church take the same preceding quick examination. Take the scores of the leaders, and average them together. How are you doing as a team? What can you do to improve that score?
4. Consider the feasibility of using the Attitude Quotient with the entire congregation. Before you do this, consider what responses you think you will receive. After taking it, what sorts of results were reported on a personal, leadership and church-wide level? Develop an action plan to determine what you can do in the next few days, weeks and months to grow and encourage new attitudes in your congregation.
5. Begin a series of sermons or lessons to send the message to your church that God directs the work of the church. To be a part of God's perfect plan is the most exciting and significant function that we can accomplish as human beings. The church will prevail if all of its parts are working in harmony and unity to do God's work.

Tier 2

Unity

> *Finally, be strong in the Lord, and in His mighty power. Put on the full armor of God so that you can take your stand against the devil's schemes. For our struggle is not against flesh and blood, but against the rulers, against the authorities, against the powers of this dark world and against the spiritual forces of evil in the heavenly realms.*
>
> Ephesians 6:10–12

WE'VE REACHED OUR FIRST switchback. Although that word may seem a bit strange, if you've ever driven through the mountains—or even up a very large hill—you've probably encountered one without even realizing it.

A switchback is the point (or points) along a trail or road when there is a radical reversal of direction that is almost a 180 degree turn. My kids call it a "zig-zag." My wife calls it a "*Please drive more slowly!*" point.

The reason we encourage a leadership team to use a switchback is that it is very important to take a few moments to rest and reflect. *If the church has successfully traversed the beginning ascent through Motivation, Obedience and Attitude, then things may start to get a bit different in the life of the Body.*

There is a general assumption that if we have come together on the previous three, we will automatically have achieved unity. However, while seeds will certainly have been planted, there is no doubt that at this point, the journey will take on a new spiritual dimension. The challenge of effectiveness now requires the acknowledgment of and attention to the Biblical concept of spiritual warfare.

How does spiritual warfare come into this picture?

> *Be self-controlled and alert. Your enemy the devil prowls around like a roaring lion looking for someone to devour. Resist him, standing firm in the faith, because you know that your brothers throughout the world are undergoing the same kind of sufferings.*
>
> 1 Peter 5:8–9

Christ knew full well what the Church would face when He left. In His high priestly prayer recorded in John 17, Jesus prayed for our protection from the evil one. He also prayed that we may be one. Jesus knew that disunity would be a chief weapon of our earthly enemy.

Persecution existed at the time of Christ and it still exists today. Many in the North American church have gotten very comfortable and complacent. Strong spiritual growth and movement will bring spiritual warfare to the forefront. It is important to spend significant time in the practice of the spiritual discipline of prayer before proceeding. *Pray specifically and mightily for unity.*

The level of unity consists of three components: Relationships, Communication and Structure. Understanding and applying these three components will help build tremendous unity. The church will only be successful to the extent that it can become unified behind its mission. Unity must be a daily goal. A unified church will accomplish much for the Lord. Without such togetherness, our effectiveness will be nullified.

5

Relationships

Teamwork Under Christ

Sitting in El Salvador on a patio chair overlooking the Pacific Ocean while the gentle ocean breezes gently drifted in, my friend remarked to me as we sipped lemonade, "This is what we call *Suffering for Jesus*." I laughed so hard I almost fell out of my chair. It wasn't that his statement was particularly funny. The persecuted church across the globe knows true suffering. But, at the time, it came at the end of an unusually difficult week of working with a team and doing some very physically grueling labor.

In fact, just a few days earlier, this scene would have been completely unimaginable as I'd spent those twenty-four hours alternating trips between a cot and the bathroom—battling a strange Central American parasite. However, we had just taken the team back to the airport for their return home and we were on our way back to clean up. This brief roadside respite was not on my agenda, but my friend recognized the need for both of us to stop for a minute and just rest.

Given time to reflect on that moment in my history, I cannot help but be grateful to my friend for the care he had for me. I would not have admitted the need to rest. As a "Type-A" person, my mind had already jumped ahead to the next dozen tasks we needed to accomplish. My friend however, recognized that if I didn't take a break, my energy and attitude would continue to be depleted and I'd be back in bed—this time from exhaustion.

A true friend will recognize when his or her beloved is in need of anything. Whether it is a word of encouragement, a hug, a rebuke, or simply a moment of precious time, a friend is able to recognize a need.

Friendships can obviously grow out of any number of things—struggles, loneliness, common likes (or dislikes), etc . . . —or simply out of circumstances. I find one of the most interesting relationships in Scripture to be the one between Ruth and Naomi.

For ten years, Ruth (whose name in Hebrew actually sounds like the word for friendship) had been the daughter in law of Naomi. After the death of her husband and two sons, Naomi decided to return to her native land of Bethlehem in Judah. She started out with her two daughters-in-law, Ruth and Orpah, but then decided they should return to Moab. Although Orpah decided to return home, Ruth replied with a deeply heartfelt response.

> *Don't urge me to leave you or to turn back from you. Where you go I will go, and where you stay I will stay. Your people will be my people and your God my God. Where you die I will die and there I will be buried. May the LORD deal with me, be it ever so severely, if anything but death separates you and me.*
>
> Ruth 1:16–17

Ruth was now a part of Naomi's family. Death had technically given her cause for separation, but she chose to value friendship and relationship over the security offered in returning home. She knew that Naomi needed her and she cared for Naomi. She felt the calling of God upon her heart and acted on it.

The component of "Relationships" is all about listening to God. We need to listen to God individually and corporately. We also need to pay attention to how others listen to God. As we do this, we'll look at Ruth, Boaz, Naomi and the others surrounding this brief narrative of Scripture.

GUIDING PRINCIPLE

The only separation the Bible knows is between believers on the one hand and unbelievers on the other. Any other kind of separation, division or disunity is of the devil. It is evil and from sin.

—Bishop Desmond Tutu

THE CHALLENGE OF LEADERSHIP

When it gets down to the root of effectiveness, whether it is in the church or some other group of people trying to accomplish something together, it is the quality of relationships that makes the difference. The perfect plans will be thwarted if people are not wiling to trust each other and work interdependently. Leaders must work hard to build relationships in their churches. This includes both the vertical relationships between individuals and God and the horizontal relationships between brothers and sisters in Christ.

The following key questions are important to consider as we review the component of relationships.

- Why are relationships so important to the effectiveness of the church?
- How do we grow closer to God?
- Why is prayer important to the functioning of the Body as a whole?
- How can prayer help us to be more effective leaders?
- How do we grow closer to one another as brothers and sisters in Christ?
- What are some healthy models for human interaction and effectiveness?
- How does God admonish us to protect our relationships?

- Moving through these questions and completing the exercises will help you to better grasp God's desire for us to work with Him and with one another as brothers and sisters in Christ.

WHY ARE RELATIONSHIPS SO IMPORTANT TO THE EFFECTIVENESS OF THE CHURCH?

There's just no getting around the truth of the issue. Naomi was angry with God. As we look at God's Word, we can feel the depths of her grief and the bitterness of her heart. Listen to her words as she returns home to Bethlehem and is surrounded by townspeople:

> *"Don't call me Naomi," she told them. "Call me Mara, because the Almighty has made my life very bitter. I went away full, but the LORD has brought me back empty. Why call me Naomi? The LORD has afflicted me; the Almighty has brought misfortune upon me."*
>
> Ruth 1:20–21

Now, if you heard the words, did you feel them? Did your heart break at the agony she expressed? I remember seeking to offer some words of counsel and comfort to a woman at a church. Now in her 70's, she had outlived three of her four children. Her refrain was tragic: "A parent should never outlive their children."

Naomi had lost both her sons and her husband. She had given herself over to bitterness of heart.

In many ways, the book of Ruth is *not* about Ruth. It's about Naomi. It's about her restoration from bitterness to hope. Her healing would come through relationship. Leaders in the church must work diligently to achieve healthy relationships in the church.

Good relationships are simply indispensable to the effective functioning of any organization. *Leaders will only be effective to the extent that they have the respect and trust of those they are attempting to lead.* Leadership has changed in the last several years. Dictatorial leadership is no longer accepted within the majority of organizations in North America.

True leadership cannot be assigned or elected. Trust must be gained and kept. In the Christian setting, relationship building must be intentional and consistent. This is a key component of the effective church and a most crucial component as we consider God's call to unity. Scripture, especially the New Testament, is full of exhortations challenging us to love one another and to learn to live together.

> *And the second* [Greatest Commandment] *is like it: Love your neighbor as yourself.*
>
> Matthew 22:39

> *Love must be sincere. Hate what is evil; cling to what is good. Be devoted to one another in brotherly love. Honor one another above yourselves. Never be lacking in zeal, but keep your spiritual fervor, serving the Lord. Be joyful in hope, patient in affliction, faithful in prayer. Share with God's people who are in need. Practice hospitality.*
>
> Romans 12:9–13

> *Carry each other's burdens, and in this way you will fulfill the law of Christ.*
>
> Galatians 6:2

God understood that nurturing a healthy relationship with Himself and sustaining unity among believers would be our greatest challenges as Christians.

HOW DO WE GROW CLOSER TO GOD?

Ruth had no reason to follow Naomi. Naomi told her daughters-in-law to leave. Orpah chose to return home. Ruth "clung" to her. When Naomi again told her to go to her home, Ruth replied even more strongly.

> *"Don't urge me to leave you or to turn back from you. Where you go I will go, and where you stay I will stay. Your people will be my people and your God my God. Where you die I will die, and there I will be buried. May the LORD deal with me, be it ever so severely, if anything but death separates you and me."*
>
> Ruth 1:16–17

Ruth professed the depth of her relationship and commitment to Naomi. In addition, she made these statements in the name of the Lord. This was a commitment to God as well as her mother-in-law.

Do you have that depth of commitment to God? Would you cling to Him no matter what happened in your life? I'd like to encourage you to begin implementing three key things in your life to deepen your personal relationship with God.

1. *Pray!* To stay intimately connected with God, leaders must be in touch with their Father through consistent, meaningful and intentional prayer. If leaders have any hope of effectively leading people, they must be in touch with God continuously. A man or woman that does not have a vital, life-dependent prayer life will not be effective as a leader in the church.

> *Men and women who know their God are men and women who pray, and the first point where their zeal and energy for Gods' glory come to expression is in their prayers . . . the invariable fruit of true knowledge of God is energy to pray for God's cause—energy, indeed, which can only find an outlet and a relief of inner tension when channeled into such prayer—and the more knowledge the more energy! By this we test ourselves . . . If . . . there is in us little energy for such prayer, and little consequent practice of it, this is a sure sign that as yet we scarcely know our God.*[1]

2. *Read!* To stay intimately connected with God, leaders must be in touch with their Father through consistent, meaningful and intentional study of Scripture. A key way to listen to God and to seek His instructions is to read His written word to us. A man or woman that does not have a frequent and passionate study time will not be effective as a leader in the church.

> *But as for you, continue in what you have learned and have become convinced of, because you know those from whom you learned it, and how from infancy you have known the holy Scriptures, which are able to make you wise for salvation through faith in Christ Jesus. All Scripture is God breathed and is useful for teaching, rebuking, correcting and training in righteousness, so that the man of God may be thoroughly equipped for every good work.*
>
> 2 Timothy 3:14–17

3. *Worship!* Once again, to stay intimately connected with God, leaders must be in touch with their Father through consistent, meaningful and intentional worship. Worship is to be both a communal event and a private habit. We worship corporately as we gather in prayer, praise, and proclamation of the Word and the celebration of the sacraments. We wor-

---

1. J. I. Packer, *Knowing God*, Intervarsity Press, 1993.

ship God alone in prayer, study, and songs of praise. Our very lives are to be lived on a daily basis as if we are worshipping God. Work, in church or out, should be an act of worship and thanksgiving to God.

> *Let us draw near to God with a sincere heart in full assurance of faith . . . Let us hold unswervingly to the hope we profess for He who promised is faithful. And let us consider how we may spur one another on toward love and good deeds. Let us not give up meeting together, as some are in the habit of doing, but let us encourage one another—and all the more as you see the Day approaching.*
>
> Hebrews 10:22–25

WHY IS PRAYER IMPORTANT TO THE FUNCTIONING OF THE BODY AS A WHOLE?

> *Without prayer, a church is like a body without a spirit; it is a dead, inanimate thing. A church with prayer in it has God in it. When prayer is set aside, God is outlawed. When prayer becomes an unfamiliar exercise, then God Himself is a stranger there.*[2]

The preceding quote answers the question perfectly. E. M. Bounds has eloquently captured the essence of the necessity of prayer in the church.

Two kinds of prayer are important to the functioning of the Body as a whole: individual and corporate. If the individuals in the pews are not praying, they are not enjoying the benefits of a deep relationship with their Savior. If the church is not praying together, their fellowship is lacking an intimate way to stay connected to each other and to God. As Bounds continues:

> *As God's house is a house of prayer, prayer should enter into and underlie everything that is done there. Prayer belongs to every sort of work relating to the Church. As God's house is a house where the business of praying is carried on, so is it a place where the business of making praying people out of prayer-less people is done. The house of God is a divine workshop, and there the work of prayer goes on.*[3]

---

2. Bounds, Edward M. *Necessity of Prayer*. Christian Focus Publications, 2007.
3. Ibid.

Prayer needs to be continual in the church. Prayer needs to be continual in the life of the believer. It is key to a deep and growing relationship with God. Bounds effectively summarizes through these words:

> *Any church that calls itself the house of God but fails to magnify and teach the great lesson of prayer, should change the name of its building to something other than a church.*[4]

HOW DOES PRAYER HELP US TO BE MORE EFFECTIVE LEADERS?

I am not a big fan of winter. While I love the beauty after a snowfall, the crispness of the air and the faces of my children as we breathlessly play in the snow, I loathe the scraping of ice off car windows, shoveling snow and the dirty mush created on the roadside by the salt and sand. It seems as if I need to constantly refill the windshield washer fluid because of the amount of fluid I need to use to clean the grime that builds up. Even after spraying, and wiping, it seems that there are always streaks remaining. This is a problem not even new blades can fix.

In the same way that my vision is distorted by that filth, our spiritual eyes are often covered with the messes of the world. Living in a world of sin, we can lose sight of eternity ever waiting. Alarm bells ring. Sirens blare. Horns shatter the silence. The phone rings. Your shoelace breaks. Coffee spills on your shirt. A traffic jam made you late. The stock market dips yet again. There was another murder across town.

Sit still for a minute. Breathe deeply. Do it again. Tune out the noises. Is there a peace around you as you just sit? Can you not feel the yearning in your heart for something more? From the depths of your soul, aren't you passionately crying out for the embrace of your loving Father? This is why we pray.

If the local church had to eliminate all but one ministry that it performs, to be most effective, the one ministry remaining should be prayer. Leaders must be in prayer. Leaders must teach prayer. There is nothing more important that the church does. Prayer is not to be relegated to an occasional event or a random happenstance. Prayer must be intentional and consistent. God works. We pray.

---

4. Ibid.

* * * * *

You may be wondering: "What about Naomi and Ruth? Where are the accounts of them praying to God?" Scripture does not record their prayers. Does that mean they didn't pray? I don't think so.

I mentioned earlier that in many ways, the book of Ruth is really about Naomi as much as it is about Ruth. In chapter one, Naomi proclaims her own personal bitterness. When she returns to Bethlehem, Naomi proclaims that God has "afflicted" her. The root of this word means "good for nothing." And yet, she still sought to give the Lord's blessing to her daughters-in-law. She still offers the Lord's blessing to Boaz (Ruth 2:19–20).

I believe there is a clear and open channel of communication between God and Naomi. Naomi is wounded, yet yearning. She is aching, yet reaching.

I cannot say this more simply: *effective leaders are open.* They are willing to open up about their pain as well as their blessings. In so doing, they model for those around them how they can and should move forward in hope. Let's talk about this more with the next question.

HOW DO WE GROW CLOSER TO ONE ANOTHER AS BROTHERS AND SISTERS IN CHRIST?

In Israel, a man could sell himself, his family or his land. However, in order to protect the extended family line, a close relative could keep the property within the clan (see Leviticus 25:23–28 and 39–43). This person was called the "kinsman-redeemer."

It was a little trickier when a married man died with no sons and a widow was left behind. In principle, the redeemer was to take the widow as his wife. However, the firstborn son would then carry on the name of the one who died. If that was the only son, a situation could result in the estate of the redeemer going to the other line. This is why the closest kinsman-redeemer in Ruth said:

> *"Then I cannot redeem it because I might endanger my own estate. You redeem it yourself. I cannot do it."*
>
> Ruth 4:6

Was Boaz risking the same thing? Yes. Just as Ruth risked everything to follow Naomi, Boaz's kindness to the women exceeded any potential trepidation of a possible loss.

As difficult as it is to say, we do have to put ourselves at risk in the Church. Leaders especially have to be willing to be open. To be clear, this needs to be done with wisdom and discernment. Nevertheless, a false front of perfection will not help the Body to grow.

Relationships are critical to the smooth operation of the Body of Christ. As we work together efficiently, there will be success in our work. The Bible consistently exhorts us to unity, to be of like mind and to agree on a common cause.

> *The central idea in Christian organizations is this—the unity of the body in Christ. All management techniques, programs, church growth formulas and other efforts to advance the work of the Kingdom fall flat if we are unable to find strength and encouragement from being united with other believers in Christ.*[5]

WHAT IS THE HEALTHY MODEL FOR HUMAN INTERACTION?

Consider for a moment the interactions between Boaz and his workers.

> *Just then Boaz arrived from Bethlehem and greeted the harvesters, "The LORD be with you!" "The LORD bless you!" they called back. Boaz asked the foreman of his harvesters, "Whose young woman is that?" The foreman replied, "She is the Moabitess who came back from Moab with Naomi. She said, 'Please let me glean and gather among the sheaves behind the harvesters.' She went into the field and has worked steadily from morning till now, except for a short rest in the shelter." So Boaz said to Ruth, "My daughter, listen to me. Don't go and glean in another field and don't go away from here. Stay here with my servant girls. Watch the field where the men are harvesting, and follow along after the girls. I have told the men not to touch you. And whenever you are thirsty, go and get a drink from the water jars the men have filled." . . . As she got up to glean, Boaz gave orders to his men, "Even if she gathers among the sheaves, don't embarrass her. Rather, pull out some stalks for her from the bundles and leave them for her to pick up, and don't rebuke her."*
>
> Ruth 2:4–9; 15–16

---

5. Gangel, Kenneth, *Feeding and Leading*. Baker Books, 2000.

First, Boaz took the time to greet those working in the fields. It was a greeting of blessing—not a request for a status report. The harvesters responded with a similar greeting. Next, Boaz noticed that there was someone different among the workers. That means that Boaz took the time to look at those who were working. Finally, Boaz trusted his workers. He gave them instructions to take care of Ruth.

How can you apply this to your church as you are seeking to develop healthy models of interaction?

The church is a community. If the church is true to Biblical mandates, it is a community of believers whose priority is caring for each other and nurturing relationships. Effective churches understand this model.

> *Highly effective churches usually identify spiritual renewal as the ultimate goal of the relationships developed within the church network. Their perspective is that believers are to know, love and serve each other—just as we are to know, love and serve God Himself. To do so requires a purposeful and long-term commitment to relationships with other believers. The church, as the unifying organization, merely becomes the repository through which serious faith-based relationships emerge and are nurtured. Consequently, the local church can be defined not through its programs, buildings, events staff or teaching, but through the cumulative web of relationships that have been initiated and maintained among those who associate with that organization.*[6]

We suggest that churches strongly encourage members to be connected on three different, yet very important levels:

1. Celebration Groups—Celebration occurs as we worship together as a family in the faith. These groups are held together by a unity of belief and purpose in the One whom they are celebrating. Although a worship service can occur with groups of almost any size, seventy or more is typical.

2. Community Groups—Teaching classes or ministry efforts occur when smaller sized groups (seventeen to seventy) gather together to focus on a key issue or effort. Friendships are key to holding these groups together.

3. Care Groups—Small groups are necessary in churches as we seek to deepen the intimacy and interdependence of the individuals.

---

6. Barna, George, *Habits of Highly Effective Churches*. Gospel Light, 2001.

We want these to happen regularly with groups in sizes of seven to seventeen people.

It is through these groups that we develop healthy, caring relationships.

HOW DOES GOD ADMONISH US TO PROTECT OUR RELATIONSHIPS?

One of the greatest mysteries of the Christian life comes as we try to determine our role in the eternal scope of things. Where do we fit in? The conclusion of the book of Ruth includes a lineage of David. Interestingly, it begins with a man named Perez.

> *Then Naomi took the child, laid him in her lap and cared for him. The women living there said, "Naomi has a son." And they named him Obed. He was the father of Jesse, the father of David. This, then, is the family line of Perez:*
>
> *Perez was the father of Hezron,*
> *Hezron the father of Ram,*
> *Ram the father of Amminadab,*
> *Amminadab the father of Nahshon,*
> *Nahshon the father of Salmon,*
> *Salmon the father of Boaz,*
> *Boaz the father of Obed,*
> *Obed the father of Jesse,*
> *and Jesse the father of David.*
>
> Ruth 4:16–22

Who was Perez? To find the answer, we need to look back at Genesis chapter 38. (This chapter is a strange "break" in the account of Joseph but has incredible significance as you look at the complete Biblical tapestry!)

Let's take a quick snapshot summary. Judah had three sons. The firstborn, Er, was married to a woman named Tamar. Er was wicked and the Lord put him to death. Judah commanded his second son to lay with Tamar so that Er's line would be continued. However, he did not fulfill this responsibility, so the Lord put him to death also. Judah then had Tamar live as a widow in his house—promising her that the third son would fulfill the responsibility when he was older. However, he really didn't want to risk losing a third son.

Tamar then tricked Judah. She pretended to be a prostitute so Judah would lie with her. When she later became pregnant, Judah's first response was to kill her. However, when she proved that Judah was the father, he proclaimed:

> "She is more righteous than I, since I wouldn't give her to my son Shelah." And he did not sleep with her again.
>
> Genesis 38:26

Tamar was pregnant with two sons. As she was giving birth, one stuck out his hand and a string was tied around his wrist. However, the hand went back and the other child was born. Who was that one who "broke out?" You guessed it—Perez!

* * * * *

Now, remember that we began this section with an additional question—*Where do I fit in?* Do you think Judah ever would have imagined that Perez would have been the one to be so important in the lineage of David and eventually the Messiah Himself? I highly doubt it!

As Christians, we know that God has a plan. And we know He has designated us to be a part of that plan. Sometimes we have no idea what this will mean. We are focused on the here and now rather than considering God's eternal perspective. As His children, we are called to be His instruments. He promises us the power to get the job done.

Reality check—if that is the scope of our spiritual purpose as outlined in Scripture, how does it flesh out? How can sinful, selfish human beings ever attain a level of relationship with one another that will allow them to work interdependently with mutual trust, diligence and commonality of purpose?

Paul's epistle to the Ephesians is often referred to as the "procedure manual" for the church. The first three chapters clearly define our position in Christ Jesus. The next three chapters tell us how we are to function as the church. The bridge between the two sections is illustrative. Ephesians chapter three ends as follows:

> Now to him who is able to do immeasurably more than all we ask or imagine, according to his power that is at work within us, to him be glory in the church and in Christ Jesus throughout all generations, for ever and ever! Amen.

Ephesians 3:20-21

As the church, we have been promised the power to accomplish more for God than we can imagine. How does this happen? How can Christians appropriate this kind of power and be all that God is calling us to be? How can we insure that we are pleasing God?

We need to protect our relationships and honor them in a Christ-like manner.

The key to our power and effectiveness as the "Body of Christ," is clearly defined in the next three chapters of Ephesians, and more specifically in chapter four.

> *As a prisoner for the Lord, then, I urge you to live a life worthy of the calling you have received. Be completely humble and gentle; be patient, bearing with one another in love. Make every effort to keep the unity of the Spirit through the bond of peace.*

Ephesians 4:1-3

Christians are called to a different way of living. Our strength and power come with the unity of our efforts as we work to accomplish God's plan as a community of believers. It is this unity that will assure our success. Ephesians 4, and many others of Paul's epistles tell us how we are to live. Each individual must take these inspired admonishments and instructions to heart. We have the power to change one person in our lives. That person is our self.

As we each determine to live each day "in a manner worthy of our calling," Christ's purposes will be accomplished through us and in turn through our churches. The alternative is also clearly defined in Scripture:

> *The entire law is summed up in a single command: "Love your neighbor as yourself." If you keep on biting and devouring each other, watch out or you will be destroyed by each other.*

Galatians 5:14-15

Action Steps:

1. In the same way you completed the examination in the preceding chapter, take the quick quiz on the next page. How can the scores improve?
   - Average the score for yourself.
   - Average the score among the other leaders.
   - Average the score among the entire church.
2. Form and / or encourage an active prayer chain and regular prayer meeting time within the church. Stress the importance of these ministries and call for members to attend as consistently as they would any other event in the church.
3. Develop a prayer card system to be used Sunday morning at worship and other meeting times. (Be sure to allow for private versus public requests.)
4. Emphasize from the pulpit and in every classroom setting the desire for unity in the body of Christ. Disunity is the tool of Satan and there is no greater threat to the powers of darkness than a church with healthy relationships.
5. Begin a Christian character teaching policy in all classes. We all need reminders regarding what it means to live a Christ-like life on a daily basis. Use Ephesians 4 and Galatians 5:16–26 to give a clear rendering of Godly characteristics.

Excited = 5 Hopeful = 4 Ambivalent = 3 Worried = 2 Pessimistic = 1

  a. Personal Prayer Life:

  ___ 1. I believe that prayer should be an important part of my personal walk with Jesus Christ.

  ___ 2. I allocate some time each day devoted only to prayer and meditation.

  ___ 3. I believe that God hears and answers my prayers.

___ 4. I have concrete examples in my life where God has very specifically answered my prayers.

___ 5. I believe that my life is better and more peaceful when I am intentionally spending time each day in prayer.

___ 6. There are people in my life who do not know the Lord Jesus Christ for whom I pray on a daily basis.

___ 7. I pray for my pastor on a daily basis.

___ 8. I pray for the leaders of my church on a daily basis.

___ 9. I believe that my prayers will make a difference in the effectiveness and impact of our church.

___ 10. I believe that my prayer life is maturing at this stage of my life.

b. Prayer Ministries of My Church:

___ 1. Our church is a praying church.

___ 2. We have a specific committee or team in our church devoted to prayer.

___ 3. We believe that prayer is the most important ministry of our church.

___ 4. When I am in need of intercessory prayer, I know exactly who to contact.

___ 5. We have a strong prayer chain through which I can report my prayer needs.

___ 6. We have a system set up that reports back to us the answers to prayers that we have offered up as a congregation.

___ 7. We occasionally have Sunday School Classes or special events that deal with the subject of prayer.

___ 8. Prayer is a critical part of my Small Group Meetings.

___ 9. I would like my church to help me gain a better understanding of prayer and its place in my life.

___ 10. I would like to commit to more involvement in our prayer ministries.

6

Communication

Talking Through the Boss

"What we've got here, is failure, to communicate."

When the movie, *Cool Hand Luke*, released in theaters over thirty years ago, I wonder if Paul Newman and Stuart Rosenberg anticipated the impact of the film? Much of Newman's character is a mystery. We simply see that he refuses to submit. From a loss of rank in the army to being horrifically beaten by George Kennedy, Newman continues to battle for independence and solitude. Even when he achieves hero-like leadership status among the other prisoners, he argues to be left alone.

Although it was not a Christian film, one of the concluding scenes of the film was especially poignant. Newman has escaped yet one more time and is now hiding in a church. Repeatedly irreverent to God, he now pleads for freedom. This freedom is granted—simply not the way Newman desired.

We've now reached the middle point of our journey in the level of unity. Like Newman's character Luke, we may be at the point of pleading to God for things to happen. This is understandable. As anticipation builds, we want to see progress and see it now! We want to see the immediate rather than continuing to progressively build towards the enactment of God's plan.

Stay true!

Yes, it is frustrating to serve in any capacity in the church. Sometimes it is just a big old pain in the rumpus. There—I've said it. Don't you feel better? I know I do!

There is no Plan B.

Why then is Plan A so irritatingly hard? The answer is one simple three-letter word: SIN. Aside from wanting to let you know I have a remarkable grasp of the obvious, why do you think I bothered to say that? As we are talking about unity, we need to realize how vitally important relationships truly are to have and maintain with one another. We also need to learn how to talk with one another. We need to know how to communicate.

Let's look to God's Word and the prophet Jeremiah for some ideas.

* * * * *

> *Before I formed you in the womb I knew you, before you were born I set you apart; I appointed you as a prophet to the nations. Now, I have put my words in your mouth. See, today I appoint you over nations and kingdoms to uproot and tear down, to destroy and overthrow, to build and to plant.*
>
> Jeremiah 1:5, 9b–10

Before Jeremiah's cells began to form, before he breathed his first breath, before he took his first steps, God chose him to serve. Not only did God choose him, he appointed him as a prophet with incredibly powerful messages. God's own words would flow from Jeremiah's mouth as a means of warning people of the impending events.

God also commanded Jeremiah to do some pretty strange things as a prophet. We'll discuss some of these later in this chapter. But for now, it's important for us to realize that the methods of communication we choose are very important. We can communicate data (whether thoughts, messages or information) through various delivery systems (speech, signals, writing or behavior). As leaders, we must understand these various dynamics in order to be effective. Good leaders must be good communicators. Good communicators are sensitive to their audience regarding how messages should be sent and if (and how) messages are being received. Christ taught the crowds in parables constantly (Matthew 13:34) so that those God gave ears to hear would understand the message He was teaching.

The tongue is a mighty instrument of both edification and destruction. God calls us to use our tongues wisely in an edifying manner, doing no harm.

> *LORD, who may dwell in your sanctuary? Who may live on your holy hill? He whose walk is blameless and does what is righteous, who speaks the truth from his heart and has no slander on his tongue, who does his neighbor no wrong and casts no slur on his fellowman . . .*
>
> Psalm 15:1–3

Restraint in our speech is a Godly virtue. Rarely does a person regret holding his or her tongue. We must learn to engage our minds before we engage our speech. Our tongues should be instruments of building up one another rather than tearing down. This building up edifies the Body of Christ.

> *Do not let any unwholesome talk come out of your mouths, but only what is helpful for building others up according to their needs, that it may benefit those who listen.*
>
> Ephesians 4:29

Our new condition in Christ gives us a remarkable power to rise above the sinful ways of our old self and allows us to conduct ourselves in a new manner. Christians are to *act and react* differently than the world. There are things that we are to do and there are things that we are not to do. Gossip, false witness, rumors, half-truths and innuendos have no place in the church. We have been renewed and we need to put on a Christ-like attitude in all that we say and do.

Work in the church is frustrating. The depth of our walk is reflected in our verbal self-control. Is the Lord speaking to you or through you?

GUIDING PRINCIPLE

Seek first to understand, then to be understood.
—St. Francis of Assisi

THE CHALLENGE OF LEADERSHIP

The potential for success in any organization can be determined by analyzing the systems that have been set up to insure healthy communication between its constituents *and* the extent to which those systems are being used. Leaders must be aware of the tremendous impact that communication has on the church. Good communication systems and the diligent use of those systems can be the main factor contributing to church effectiveness. To the contrary, poor communication systems and implementation are killing churches every day. Attention to good communication by leaders in the church is critical.

A church that has struggled through the steps of developing a unified team with a common mission must strive to achieve and retain unity. Relationships are crucial and effective communication between relationships is essential. In consideration of the elements of effective communication, we will address the following questions:

1. How is the importance of communication emphasized in the Bible?
2. What is the spiritual impact of communication on unity in the church?
3. What are the channels of communication that need to be in place?
4. What are the core components of healthy communication?
5. What are the dynamics of communication in the church?
6. How is communication an issue of sensitivity for leaders?

Let us now forget those words from *Cool Hand Luke*: "*What we have here is a failure to communicate.*" We must keep this from being a common mindset in churches today. Addressing the elements of effective communication and using them to build unity will help strengthen and build your church.

HOW IS THE IMPORTANCE OF COMMUNICATION EMPHASIZED IN THE BIBLE?

The greatest mistake made in communication is found in one little word—"assume." We often make assumptions that because we say, write, or think something, others will understand it exactly as we intended them to understand.

This is wrong!

Communication is difficult. Sin exists. What we intend to say is not necessarily heard. How we intend it to be received is not necessarily the way it happens. Those things we said, didn't connect. In the book of Jeremiah, we read:

> *Hear this, you foolish and senseless people, who have eyes but do not see, who have ears but do not hear.*

Jeremiah 5:21

In context, this is specifically written to sinful Judah for forsaking the Lord. But I think the verse perfectly illustrates the essence of poor communication. We see—but we don't see. We hear—but we don't hear. Before we go too much farther down this road, let's take a step back and address the question of communication in the Bible.

* * * * *

First and foremost, Scripture is communication. The Bible itself is God's tool for communicating to people today. Jesus Christ is literally the embodiment of God's communication to us. John 1:1 refers to Jesus Christ as the Word. He was both messenger *and* message.

Scripture is overflowing with God's attempts to communicate to His children. He has even set the heavens to proclaim His glory and creation.

> *The heavens declare the glory of God; the skies proclaim the work of His hands. Day after day they pour forth speech; night after night*

> *they display knowledge. There is no speech or language where their voice is not heard. Their voice goes out into all the earth, their words to the ends of the world.*
>
> Psalm 19:1–4b

The spiritual impact of effective communication is expressed through the Tower of Babel. It is clear through this account that God understands the powerful implications of people and their ability to clearly communicate.

> *Now the whole world had one language and a common speech. As men moved eastward, they found a plain in Shinar and settled there. They said to each other, "Come, let's make brick and bake them thoroughly. They used brick instead of stone, and tar for mortar. Then they said, "Come, let us build ourselves a city, with a tower that reaches to the heavens, so that we may make a name for ourselves and not be scattered over the face of the whole earth." But the LORD came down to see the city and the tower that the men were building. The LORD said, "If as one people speaking the same language they have begun to do this, then nothing they plan will be impossible for them. Come let us go down and confuse their language so they will not understand each other." So the LORD scattered them from there over all the earth, and they stopped building the city.*
>
> Genesis 11:1–8

The ramifications in this passage are tremendous. When we are truly communicating, there is nothing that we cannot do within God's plan. In the account of the Tower, the communication and effectiveness of the people was leading to something contrary to God's plan. God stopped their sin by destroying their ability to communicate and scattered people all over the earth. This served to further His Kingdom and His plan.

WHAT IS THE SPIRITUAL IMPACT OF COMMUNICATION ON UNITY IN THE CHURCH?

As we grasp the relationship between good communication and effectiveness, we must focus on enhancing and protecting good lines of communication. A good example of the strategic use of communication can be represented in the history of military conflicts. In 1990 and again in 1998, allied military forces were called upon to suppress material threats in Iraq and Kosovo. Understanding the correlation between good communication and strategic effectiveness, the first thing that the American forces did was to destroy the enemy's ability to communicate. When we cannot communicate effectively, we cannot accomplish our work.

Jeremiah sought fervently to communicate the desperate plight the nation of Judah was going to face. In return, he was often labeled as one who was bringing a false message from the Lord. He was punished by those who opposed his messages from God.

> *Then the officials said to the king, "This man should be put to death. He is discouraging the soldiers who are left in this city, as well as all the people, by the things he is saying to them. This man is not seeking the good of these people but their ruin." "He is in your hands," King Zedekiah answered. "The king can do nothing to oppose you." So they took Jeremiah and put him into the cistern of Malkijah, the king's son, which was in the courtyard of the guard. They lowered Jeremiah by ropes into the cistern; it had no water in it, only mud, and Jeremiah sank down into the mud.*
>
> Jeremiah 38:4–6

We all like to hear good news. But hearing something we don't like can be frustrating or cause anger. The "opposition" to Jeremiah's message viewed him as a traitor because they did not believe God would allow this to happen to them—in spite of their knowledge of the sin of the people.

There are human reasons why communication can fail. But there are also spiritual reasons. The apostle Peter gave us one important spiritual reason why communication fails.

> *Be self-controlled and alert. Your enemy the devil prowls around like a roaring lion looking for someone to devour.*
>
> 1 Peter 5:8

Peter was well aware of the impact Satan could have on his own life.

> *Simon, Simon, Satan has asked to sift you as wheat. But I have prayed for you, Simon, that your faith may not fail. And when you have turned back, strengthen your brothers.*
>
> Luke 22:31–32

Satan understands that the church can be paralyzed by broken and misdirected communication. His work is to destroy unity and foster distrust. He is a master at his art. He does not hesitate to do whatever he can whenever he can to block us from working with one another. The leadership of every church must be on guard against disunity, damage to relationships and communication failures. Leaders must be on their knees in prayer for themselves and for their fellow leaders. Only after we are united on our *knees*, can we begin to *stand* together in unity.

When a church has embraced its mission, when it is motivated, obedient and has a Godly attitude, its potential for remarkable success is established. That potential will only be realized as the church stands unified. However, we must be ever vigilant.

WHAT ARE THE CHANNELS OF COMMUNICATION THAT NEED TO BE IN PLACE?

The channel of communication that must be in place is between an individual and God. The communication between an individual believer and the Creator is crucial to one's walk. Without talking to the One who gave us life, we cannot hope to live the abundant life!

Healthy communication in the church at the functional level is dependent on two-way communication between at least three specific groups. In most church settings, the groups include the professional staff, the lay leadership and the congregation. To keep each of the church's constituencies "in sync," intentional effort is required to make sure that channels of communication have been established for both sending and receiving information. Of course, there needs to be good communication within each of these groups as well.

The key is establishing channels of communication that everyone in the church understands. If there is a conflict between staff members, what route should pursued? Should two members of the church enter into a dispute, how should that dispute be resolved (especially in accordance with Matthew 18:15–17)? How are different ministries able to get their own messages out to the congregation at large?

In addition, the use of these channels of communication needs to be consistently encouraged and sanctioned. Communication is an on-going process—not a singular event. The life of the church is dependent on healthy channels of communication.

Evaluation of these channels of communication is also a necessary step to effectiveness. The church that is struggling within its ministries or in its relationships may need to take a step back and evaluate their communication channels. Sometimes, to truly become effective communicators, it may even take an objective third party to observe and recommend changes.

Remember that God had Jeremiah use a multitude of symbols to communicate. From a ruined belt (chapter 13) and a smashed jar (chapter 19) to a yoke (chapter 27) and large stones (chapter 43), he sought to communicate God's message in ways people would see and understand.

Sometimes we have to be exceptionally creative. Sometimes we need to go back to the basics and begin with the core essentials.

WHAT ARE THE CORE COMPONENTS OF HEALTHY COMMUNICATION?

My friends and I had to walk to elementary school. When we arrived early, we would get together with other students and play tag. One morning, as we were running on the side of the building, I slipped in the dew-wet grass and slid partially through a ground-level basement window.

Some friends carefully helped me escape the sharp glass remains and took me to the school office. On hearing that I had crashed through a window, rather than inquiring about my cuts and providing some bandages, the administrator told me I was going to have to pay for damages. It wasn't exactly what anyone expected to hear!

All the administrator had heard was that I had broken a window. Until a group came over to look at the area, they hadn't really even considered the potential hazard. The rather frantic explanations from semi-coherent ten year-olds didn't penetrate.

To understand healthy communication, it is as simple as looking back to childhood. Communication can be represented by two cans and a string. It is all we need to get a message from one person to another. The two cans represent:

- A place where the message originates (sender)
- A vehicle for transferring the message between the sender and the recipient (delivery system)
- A place where the message is to be received (receiver)

Obviously, the components are quite simple. The dynamics however, are a much more critical phenomenon.

WHAT ARE THE DYNAMICS OF COMMUNICATION IN THE CHURCH?

About a year later, I was playing with some friends in our neighborhood. We were racing from one yard to another and then across a street. As I ran out from between two parked cars, I was hit by a passing car.

As I lay in the street, my friends ran back to my house to get help. My older brother answered the door. Upon hearing their yells, he angrily started to close the door in their faces, muttering, "*Yeah right. April Fool's.*" (Did I forget to mention that it was April 1st?) However, he quickly realized by their frantic expressions and continued pleas that it was not a joke. Help was summoned and I was able to experience my first ride in an ambulance.

I bring up these examples from my childhood not to regale you with youthful exploits of accidents and danger, but in an attempt to return you to the basics of communication. Somehow, we seem to forget these things as we age and overcomplicate a simple process.

If the representation of communication is as simple as two cans and a string, why do we so often have a breakdown in communication? The point where the message is sent and the point where the message is received are too often in conflict. There are several opportunities for this breakdown to occur.

1. *Message never sent*—In the church, it is incredibly damaging to unity. While we can attempt to justify things, messages are not sent for several reasons, including:

    - Innocent negligence—"We simply forgot to tell you."
    - Habitual insensitivity—"I didn't realize you would be interested in this."
    - Flagrant malicious intent—"They don't need to know."

2. *Wrong message sent*—"We had no idea that this meeting was to be as important as it turned out to be."

3. *Wrong delivery system used*—"I heard you put the information in the bulletin last week, but we were out of town last week."

4. *Message recipient not listening*—"There is so much irrelevant information in the bulletin each week, that we have trained ourselves not to read any of it."

5. *Wrong message received*—"We know that's what you said, but we know your motives and how you operate. That's not what you meant."

Obviously, with so many opportunities for breakdown, communication channels must be worked on very carefully. In marketing efforts, the standard is three vehicles. Tell them once, tell them again and then tell them one more time. Often, the vehicle itself will vary as well. It is typical to reach out to the auditory learners through verbal messages (radio, television, word of mouth, etc . . .) as well as the visual learners through written messages (newspapers, magazines, billboards, etc . . .).

In the church, we need to remember both the many potential messages and the various receiving styles that exist. Is this important enough to put in the already full bulletin or might it cause other items to be missed? Does it necessitate a direct word from the pastor? Should it be communicated through Sunday School classes or small groups? Would a poster(s) be appropriate? Is your church "wired" for email messages to congregants? Our goal needs to be *effective communication*. Our vehicle therefore should be consistent to achieve our goal.

HOW IS COMMUNICATION AN ISSUE OF SENSITIVITY FOR LEADERS?

Jeremiah would never have been accused of being the life of the party. In fact, Jeremiah wasn't even allowed to go to the party! Immediately after God prohibits Jeremiah from going to funerals, he commands him not to go to houses where there is feasting.

> *"And do not enter a house where there is feasting and sit down to eat and drink." For this is what the LORD Almighty, the God of Israel, says: "Before your eyes and in your days I will bring an end to the sounds of joy and gladness and to the voices of bride and bridegroom in this place."*
>
> Jeremiah 16:8–9

Jeremiah, often referred to as the "Weeping Prophet," was used by God to bring a difficult message to the people. Because of this, he appears to have few friends. Although King Josiah followed the Lord, when he died (see 2nd Chronicles 35:20–25), Jeremiah was not liked by subsequent kings. In fact, Jehoiakim cut up and then burned a scroll from Jeremiah piece by piece! (Jeremiah 36:20–23)

Good communication is intentional. It is done with a clear purpose or direction in mind. Successful communication happens when there is mutual trust. We need to constantly be considering the importance of our messages, the listening propensity of our audience and the appropriate methods of delivery. Messages sent that are not properly received are often worse than messages that are never sent at all.

Communication is as much an art as it is a science. It takes a wise leader to grasp the necessity of continuously improving the vehicles of communication. It takes an ever-vigilant leader to understand his or her people and their readiness and openness to be led. Good communication is the key.

> *If words are to enter men's hearts and bear fruit, they must be the right words, shaped cunningly to pass men's defenses and explode silently and effectually in their minds.*
>
> —J. B. Phillips

Simply building systems and launching them will not be enough. The systems and encouragement to use them must be sustained. Communication will deteriorate if left unattended. This is our nature.

* * * * *

I'd like to add a final note to this important chapter. I hope the importance of effective communication has been sufficiently stressed. Nevertheless, communication is simply one of the most potentially damaging and explosive aspects of ministry. It is also potentially one of the most powerful methods of blessing.

I'd like to give you some hope. Jeremiah also brought a message of the promise of restoration to the people.

> "This is what the LORD says: As I have brought all this great calamity on this people, so I will give them all the prosperity I have promised them. Once more fields will be bought in this land of which you say, 'It is a desolate waste, without men or animals, for it has been handed over to the Babylonians.' Fields will be bought for silver, and deeds will be signed, sealed and witnessed in the territory of Benjamin, in the villages around Jerusalem, in the towns of Judah

and in the towns of the hill country, of the western foothills and of the Negev, because I will restore their fortunes, declares the LORD."

Jeremiah 32:42–44

God promises hope. God fulfills His promises. No matter what has gone on in the past, there is *hope for the future*. As we collectively turn to the Lord and seek His wisdom and direction, we will find that He will supply our needs. We must do all things through His strength.

Action Steps:

1. It is critical that a church understand its different constituencies and that it develop and maintain channels of communication between them. Channels must provide for two-way communication. Consider for yourself (and as a team) the various channels of communication and their effectiveness in both sending *and* receiving.
   - Pastor & Staff to Lay Leadership
   - Pastor & Staff to Congregation
   - Lay Leadership to Congregation

2. Evaluate the understanding of your church at large regarding the channels of communication. Solicit input from the congregation regarding their opinion of communication in the church. What is effective and what is not? What new ideas do they have for communicating? In what ways can they take ownership of these ideas?

3. Create a structure for evaluating all communication in a given time period (two weeks or a month—depending on the church size). What succeeded? What communication / methods of communication could have been eliminated? Could any of it have been shortened (brevity often increases likelihood of being read)?

4. Go high-tech. Consider the future possibilities of technology for email broadcasting and web site use. As more homes and businesses become "wired," the ease of effectively and quickly communicating will be phenomenally increased. Once again, consider the gifts and talents of those in your church. For which person could this become a ministry?

7

Structure

Who's the Boss?

Order. Chaos. Arrangement. Mix-up. Sequential. Muddle. Which words make you think of God? Any student of Scripture will know that God is a God of order. From the beginning of all things, God has had in place a plan and a structure for accomplishing His perfect will. His plan is perfect. Will our plans be perfect? Probably not . . .

I have often been described as a Type-A person. I like order. However, this unfortunately often results in control issues. It can be tough to release things in spite of the capableness and talent of so many people around me. Although I am getting better, I often don't even see the problems I am causing myself (and others) until I am overwhelmed with too much "busyness."

Once again, God, in His wisdom, has provided me with my own personal lesson from Scripture. (Does it apply to you also?)

> *Moses' father-in-law replied, "What you are doing is not good. You and these people who come to you will only wear yourselves out. The work is too heavy for you; you cannot handle it alone. Listen now to me and I will give you some advice, and may God be with you. You must be the people's representative before God and bring their disputes to Him. Teach them the decrees and laws, and show them the way to live and the duties they are to perform. But select capable men from all the people—men who fear God, trustworthy men who hate dishonest gain and appoint them as officials over thousands, hundreds, fifties and tens. Have them serve as judges for the people at all times, but have them bring every difficult case to you; the simple cases they can decide themselves. That will make your load lighter, because they will share it with you. If you do this and God so*

> *commands, you will be able to stand the strain, and all these people will go home satisfied.*

Exodus 18:17–23

Think you have it rough? Moses was the leader over thousands upon thousands of people who had just left their homes and were marching through the desert. Imagine the lines of people coming to him to complain about everything.

> *My lambs are getting mixed in with someone else's flock.*
> *The children camped next to us are too rowdy.*
> *That family never cleans up their campsite.*
> *There's too much sand.*
> *Can't you do something about this sun?*

The problems must have been overwhelming!

(There is an interesting thing to note about this story. Moses, the great leader who had defeated Pharaoh through God's Power, could not solve this problem by himself. It took the wisdom of an outsider to point out what should have been obvious. Do *you* have a method in place for evaluation from an "outsider's" perspective?)

One of the guiding principles of the church is that of the *priesthood of believers*. The work that God has ordained for each church is much more than the active "20%" can handle and certainly too much for a pastor to accomplish alone. When wandering in the desert, Moses—the leader—felt the responsibility to do it all. Providentially, his father-in-law Jethro helped him to see the wisdom of delegation.

Structure may not seem very interesting or exciting, but a truly effective structure will provide blessings beyond measure. Those who serve will be happier as they use their gifts. They will be more excited as they see things happen. Ministries will be more efficient. Outreach will be more effective.

I could go on and on, but let's look at the Gospel of Matthew for a moment.

> *Therefore everyone who hears these words of mine and puts them into practice is like a wise man who built his house on the rock. The rain came down, the streams rose, and the winds blew and beat against that house; yet it did not fall, because it had its foundation on the rock.*

Matthew 7:24–25

Christ told this parable as a clear message of the wisdom of following His teaching. It is sometimes difficult to accept, but rules are actually a good thing. They protect us. They guide us. They let us know the boundaries. They help us to operate efficiently and effectively. While still being a God of love, mercy and compassion, God also teaches rules and discipline.

I read about a study conducted by psychologists several years ago. They observed children playing in a beautiful square-shaped park area. Four very busy streets on each side surrounded the park. The children all stayed in the center of the park to play on the playground structure in the center of the park—in spite of the grass available for them to run in and trees on which to climb. After observing the children for a time, they had a fence erected on the boundary of the park area. Suddenly the children were running everywhere in the park, climbing trees and even the fence!

What made the remarkable difference possible? They concluded it was simply clear boundaries. God, in His remarkable wisdom, provides us with our own set of rules in His Word so that we know exactly how far we can go and still be safe. As a church, we can operate with unlimited excitement and freedom provided we remain within His boundaries.

Do not be afraid of implementing a solid structure in the church. Many individuals fear that structure will limit the working of the Holy Spirit. Is it not incredibly egotistical to think that anything we do will prevent the Spirit from moving where He wants to move? In my experience, those who fear structure oftentimes actually fear a lack of losing control. In fact, the freedom structure provides actually opens the door for greater ministry opportunities. Hence, the Spirit will only be able to do greater things!

Structure provides us with a wonderful opportunity to serve our Creator and accomplish what He has ordained for us. Time spent developing a Godly structure for our church will both enhance and protect our unity as we work together. Rules are both a good thing *and* a God thing!

GUIDING PRINCIPLE

Be militant! Be an organization that is going to do things!

—Woodrow Wilson

THE CHALLENGE OF LEADERSHIP

The challenge of leadership in building an effective structure is not only a good thing—it is a God thing! Leaders should *not* ignore this vital component. Effective church leaders take the time to build an organizational structure that will support accomplishing the ministries that God has ordained in an efficient and productive manner. As churches grow, the development of an efficient operating structure is essential. The following questions will be discussed as we look at the development of an orderly structure.

- Why is it important to be organized as we accomplish the work of the church?
- What are the essential elements of effective leadership development?
- What are the advantages of an organizational chart?
- Why procedures and by-laws?
- What are core values and why is it important to establish them?
- How do we go about defining roles for all leadership positions?
- What is the relationship between spiritual gifts and church effectiveness?
- Why is it important to have a system for moving people through the discipleship process?

Structure will be more beneficial if it is established in anticipation of growth and the expansion of ministries rather than in response to them.

It is the responsibility of visionary leaders to put the structures in place that will support the specific plan that God has created for the church.

WHY IS IT IMPORTANT TO BE ORGANIZED AS WE ACCOMPLISH THE WORK OF THE CHURCH?

Moses. Take a few moments to think about everything you can recall about Moses.

- Where was he born?
- What were the circumstances?
- Where did he grow up?
- Who was his family?
- What influenced his life as he was growing up?
- What change caused him to leave his birthplace?
- What happened to him when he left?
- Why did he come back?
- What happened when he did?
- What changes happened to his people?
- What kind of a leader was he?
- Where did he die? (And who buried him?)

Now, I'd like you to take a few moments and reflect on the other leaders in your church. With the exception of the last question, can you answer those questions about your pastor and your fellow leaders?

In Exodus, Moses asked God a few questions as they spoke at the burning bush. One of those questions was simply this:

> *Who am I, that I should go to Pharaoh and bring the Israelites out of Egypt?*
>
> Exodus 3:11

Did you catch those first three words? "*Who am I?*" Moses was a man who had to overcome many hurdles in his life. From being condemned to die at birth to being cast into the river, his early days were certainly not the norm! He was raised as an Egyptian. He took it upon himself to attempt to lead a rebellion and killed a man in the process. And then he ran . . .

Moses spent a great deal of time in the desert. I imagine that his former life would have come back to him from time to time. After all, he'd gone from being an educated man in the most powerful nation to tending sheep. Even so, that would not have prepared him for the way his world was about to be shaken.

> *"Do not come any closer," God said. "Take off your sandals, for the place where you are standing is holy ground." Then he said, "I am the God of your father, the God of Abraham, the God of Isaac and the God of Jacob." At this, Moses hid his face, because he was afraid to look at God. The LORD said, "I have indeed seen the misery of my people in Egypt. I have heard them crying out because of their slave drivers, and I am concerned about their suffering. So I have come down to rescue them from the hand of the Egyptians and to bring them up out of that land into a good and spacious land, a land flowing with milk and honey — the home of the Canaanites, Hittites, Amorites, Perizzites, Hivites and Jebusites. And now the cry of the Israelites has reached me, and I have seen the way the Egyptians are oppressing them. So now, go. I am sending you to Pharaoh to bring my people the Israelites out of Egypt."*

Exodus 3:5–10

The reason we're spending time on these details is found in the root of the initial question: *Why is it important to be organized as we accomplish the work of the church?* Your background and experience will be different from that of your fellow leaders. Indeed, it will be different from that of each person in the church! There will be similarities and areas that overlap, but it is very important to understand how you will approach different situations. It is important that you appreciate the background that will influence the decisions of another.

A key premise for moving forward as a church is this: *God does not ask the church to do anything that He has not already given it the resources to accomplish.* As He calls you to serve Him, you can go forward knowing that He will supply your needs if it is in His pleasing and perfect will. We should therefore organize efficiently to get the most out of the resources that God has provided. An important element of this is spiritual gifts, but we will discuss that later.

*****

As we study the church, one of the most remarkable phenomena is its organizational structure. Consider the work of your church. What are the duties that need to be accomplished each week, month or quarter? Consider the basics (from cleaning to bulletin preparation) to the complex (counseling to tax reporting issues). If those who are gifted are not serving in the proper roles, it is no wonder things are difficult!

A tragic mistake is found in churches that have shifted many of the organizational responsibilities to the pastor. Is this the calling of the pastor? Is the focus of seminaries to train and develop skills in these areas? Truthfully, although some have these gifts, many pastors have reported feeling forced into the administrative arena. Churches are usually gifted with well-trained, experienced and effective leaders from highly organized and structured secular professions. The irony is that these spiritually chosen church leaders often do not transfer their leadership abilities to the church! This is an enigma that many churches need to address. The more organized, efficient and structurally balanced the church is, the more time it will have to spend on life-changing ministry rather than dulling "ministrivia."

Personally, I am not a great number cruncher. I am good at analyzing some statistical data, following trends and forecasting ahead. However, I would be bored silly by balancing a checkbook. It would take me twice as long to do it than someone who has a penchant for numbers. Therefore, wouldn't my church be foolish to put me in charge of the checkbook? Wouldn't *I* be even *more* foolish to accept that role?

The responsibility flows two ways. If the church knows someone is not gifted, that person should not be forced into a role that would be in opposition of his or her gifts. In the same light, if an individual knows that they have no business filling a certain role, they should not attempt to force themselves into accepting such a position. A square peg will simply not fit into a round hole.

WHAT ARE THE ESSENTIAL ELEMENTS OF EFFECTIVE LEADERSHIP DEVELOPMENT?

Leadership is cultivating in people today, a willingness on their part to follow you into something new for the sake of something great.

—Daniel Brown

In her book, *What the Bible is All About*, Henrietta Mears stated that D. L. Moody described Moses this way:

> *Moses spent his first forty years thinking he was somebody. He spent his second forty years learning he was a nobody. He spent his third forty years discovering what God can do with a nobody.*[1]

I don't think Moses felt ready to return to Egypt. This much is apparent from his next question to God which begins with *"Suppose I go . . ."*

> *Moses said to God, "Suppose I go to the Israelites and say to them, 'The God of your fathers has sent me to you,' and they ask me, 'What is his name?' Then what shall I tell them?"*
>
> Exodus 3:13

When Moses had asked God his previous question (Who am I?), did you notice that God didn't answer him? He simply told Moses that He would be going with him. This wasn't about Moses. This was about God redeeming His people who were crying out to Him for relief. God had chosen Moses as the man that He would use to accomplish this task.

* * * * *

If then, we have leaders in our church whom God has called, the question to answer is this: What method will we use to intentionally train our leaders how to lead? The most crucial step to assure a healthy organization is to establish a good plan and system for leadership development. The following list highlights seven essential elements involved in the effective development of leadership in the church.

- *Identify*—Choose your leaders based on God's criteria, not just the leadership criteria of the world. Make sure you give plenty of time to the process and identify and "test" potential leaders long before they might be called.
- *Enlist*—Develop a comprehensive plan and schedule for choosing your leadership and make sure that the entire congregation understands it.
- *Equip*—Make sure your potential leaders know what will be

---

1. Mears, Henrietta, *What the Bible is all About*. Regal Books, 2002.

expected of them and give them the training they need to do the job well. Jesus invested much of His time to training and equipping His core leadership team of the apostles.

- *Empower*—Give leaders real responsibility and then trust that they will get the job done well. Nothing demoralizes leaders more than receiving a job to do and then having it done for them by the one who delegated to make sure it was done "correctly."

- *Engage*—Be sure to use your leaders in a significant and effective way. The more important the job is perceived to be, the more commitment will be dedicated to it. The successful completion of jobs will engender increased confidence, the willingness to take on more assignments and future success.

- *Encourage*—Make sure your leaders understand that you will be praying for them and encouraging them as they successfully accomplish their work. Good work should always be acknowledged.

- *Evaluate*—We all need feedback. Develop a system for honestly evaluating your leaders on an on-going basis. Accountability will stimulate action.

> *There is no correlation between potential and performance. There are lots of people with potential that do nothing with it. What counts is performance. GREAT LEADERS DO SOMETHING.*
>
> —Peter Drucker

WHAT ARE THE ADVANTAGES OF AN ORGANIZATIONAL CHART?

Moses departed Mount Horeb with a fairly simple organizational chart in place. God was the boss. Moses was the next in line. Aaron was to serve as Moses' speaker. But, as we said in the introduction to this chapter, it couldn't remain that simple.

Exodus 12:37 states that there were thousands of Israelites. It was crucial that some sort of organization be given to moving these people out of Egypt and into the Promised Land. How would you have attempted such a task? (Read Numbers 2 for a remarkable system of organization of the camps under tribal banners.) The options are too numerous to count so let's consider an even simpler example.

It's Christmas Eve and your task is to put together a child's bicycle. However, the directions are missing. You know what the end result is supposed to look like, don't you? But how do you put these parts together to finish that picture-perfect image?

Much like those missing bicycle directions, the church needs to have specific directions to determine how to put things together to fulfill God's plan. In order to determine the relational structure required to get the job done, every church—no matter what size—should develop an organizational chart. The importance of such a tool will only increase exponentially as the size of the church grows. The lack of such a chart will serve only to confuse and misdirect efforts along the path.

The organizational chart performs at least two functions:

- The chart makes it very clear who reports to whom and to whom each leader, both volunteer and paid, is accountable. One of the greatest shortfalls in the structure of the church today is the lack of accountability. We don't do much simply because we are not being held accountable. Documented patterns of accountability will remedy this.

- A good organizational chart helps the congregation to know both who their present leaders are and to whom they should go with prayer requests, questions, problems or ideas. It will also let an individual know to whom to report if the Lord is calling them to serve in a specific ministry. If we are not sure who is in charge, we typically go to the pastor, increasing his burden unnecessarily.

WHY PROCEDURES AND BY-LAWS?

There are few things more mundane and seemingly less "Kingdom-building" than writing standard procedures and by-laws for the church. This is a painstaking and tedious process. But God was clear very early in the Passover covenant with the Israelites that He had expectations that must be followed.

> The LORD said to Moses and Aaron, "These are the regulations for the Passover: "No foreigner is to eat of it. Any slave you have bought may eat of it after you have circumcised him, but a temporary resi-

> dent and a hired worker may not eat of it. "It must be eaten inside one house; take none of the meat outside the house. Do not break any of the bones. The whole community of Israel must celebrate it.
>
> "An alien living among you who wants to celebrate the LORD's Passover must have all the males in his household circumcised; then he may take part like one born in the land. No uncircumcised male may eat of it. The same law applies to the native-born and to the alien living among you."

Exodus 12:43–49

The Passover was (and is) a very special ceremony of remembrance. God did not want them to treat it lightly as a common meal. In the same way, we must not treat the work of the church lightly. Procedures and by-laws give us clarity in direction and help us understand how we are to operate.

There are two important factors to remember. First, once by-laws are written, the task is *done* (except for small possible futures adjustments and minor changes). When difficult situations arise (and they will), you have prepared answers. Second, with written procedures, you now have a set template. You know the "how" as you approach a task. Relationship building and communication will be greatly enhanced with a thorough understanding of your operational procedures.

[Note—Listen to people. If something is not working or a new method is available, prayerfully consider making changes. "This is how we have always done it" can be a death sentence. Many churches have lost both people and resources due to that attitude.]

WHAT ARE CORE VALUES AND WHY IS IT IMPORTANT TO ESTABLISH THEM?

It wasn't long before the Israelites left Egypt that they ran into the first problem. Pharaoh changed his mind. Not only did he change his mind, he came after them while they were camped. The Red Sea blocked their escape!

> As Pharaoh approached, the Israelites looked up, and there were the Egyptians, marching after them. They were terrified and cried out to the LORD. They said to Moses, "Was it because there were no graves in Egypt that you brought us to the desert to die? What have you done to us by bringing us out of Egypt? Didn't we say to you in Egypt,

> *'Leave us alone; let us serve the Egyptians'? It would have been better for us to serve the Egyptians than to die in the desert!"*
>
> Exodus 14:10–12

It is stunning that the Israelites, days removed from the Passover, were ready to return to their slavery. I'm not saying that their fear wasn't understandable. I'm simply asking you to think about their values at this time.

What did they believe in? Did they really believe that God had a plan and a purpose for them? Did they really believe that their deliverance had come?

Let me ask you—What do you value? What do you *really* value? What will you *die* for? Take a few moments to think about that . . .

* * * * *

The reason I asked you to do that is so that we could set a true standard for core values. In the church, there have been splits over the color of carpet. People have argued and left over the choice of decorations in the men's restroom versus decorations in the women's restroom. People have even left over an old, faded picture being removed from a hallway.

The Egyptians had a tremendous number of "gods" they worshiped. Scholars have (I believe rightly) suggested that each of the plagues was a systematic destruction by God of the gods they worshiped. A few quick examples:

- The god of the Nile was Hopi. The plague of blood demonstrated that God was greater than Hopi.
- The god of fertility, Heqt, was torn down in the plague of frogs.
- Ra, the sun god, was shown to be weak through the plague of darkness.

God proved He was superior to each false god. Finally, through the Passover and death of the firstborn son, God showed He was greater than Pharaoh. Those things the Egyptians valued in their "gods" and leaders were proven to be nothing in comparison to Yahweh.

The generation of Israelites from Egypt had been born and raised as slaves. It is what they knew. It was ingrained in their culture. But it had *not* been ingrained in their DNA. At their core, they were God's chosen people. They were *God's CHOSEN people!* No other people group on this earth could make the same claim. But, even though they had cried out for deliverance, they did not believe it had come. They could only see slavery or death.

* * * * *

In the church of today, we need to remember that we too are God's chosen people. We have been adopted into the family and we have an inheritance that cannot be equaled. Our values should reflect this in all things. Our actions, attitudes and outlook must be driven by our values.

Ideally, core values have been long established in a church as part of their initial charter. With a bold declaration for absolute truth and Scriptural ideals, a church that boldly and bravely embraces TRUTH will attract people hungry for some clear guidelines and discipline in their lives. The unfortunate tendency is to back down or down play controversial issues for fear of turning individuals away.

The creation of a list of core values and their explanations can be an extremely difficult process for some churches. The effort to reach out without offending is a valiant effort. However, if we are so concerned with the opinions of the world, we risk being unfaithful to our Savior. In Matthew 23, Jesus presents what are commonly described as the Seven Woes. He describes the Pharisees and teachers of the law in detail as He cries out over their loss of heart over the legalism of the law. He uses terms to describe them like "brood of vipers," "blind guides," "hypocrites," "snakes," and "white-washed tombs." If your church is unwilling to stand on a foundation of truth, it is better not standing at all.

It's time to either write or evaluate the core values of your church. Take a few moments to think: *What makes us a church*? What does God command us to be and do? What makes us different from a synagogue or mosque? What makes us different from a business down the street? What if someone came to your door and said "*If you don't stop saying or doing _____, or you will have to close*?" What would make you say, "*Okay, close our doors*" and not look back?

These are your core values. Stand on them. Do not bend.

* * * * *

HOW DO WE GO ABOUT DEFINING ROLES FOR ALL LEADERSHIP POSITIONS?

During a recent anniversary celebration at a church, the keynote speaker was a member of the United States House of Representatives. Having attended seminary prior to being elected to the position, he remarked that he could not have gone into the pastoral ministry. He quipped, "It's too political. During an election, I only need to win 51% of the votes to remain in office. In the church, if only 20% of your constituents are mad at you, you're in big trouble!"

Every experienced pastor and lay leader knows the truth behind that statement. It is difficult to avoid upsetting someone in the church. As human beings, we obviously have our minor pet peeves and particular likes and dislikes. Whether we are making hamburgers or teaching God's commandments, the receivers of our communication will still process the information through their own channels.

Even Moses had difficulty with his own brother and sister when he did something they disliked.

> *Miriam and Aaron began to talk against Moses because of his Cushite wife, for he had married a Cushite. "Has the LORD spoken only through Moses?" they asked. "Hasn't he also spoken through us?" And the LORD heard this. (Now Moses was a very humble man, more humble than anyone else on the face of the earth.) At once the LORD said to Moses, Aaron and Miriam, "Come out to the Tent of Meeting, all three of you." So the three of them came out. Then the LORD came down in a pillar of cloud; he stood at the entrance to the Tent and summoned Aaron and Miriam. When both of them stepped forward, he said, "Listen to my words: When a prophet of the LORD is among you, I reveal myself to him in visions, I speak to him in dreams. But this is not true of my servant Moses; he is faithful in all my house. With him I speak face to face, clearly and not in riddles; he sees the form of the LORD. Why then were you not afraid to speak against my servant Moses?" The anger of the LORD burned against them, and he left them. When the cloud lifted from above the Tent, there stood Miriam —leprous, like snow. Aaron turned toward her and saw that she had leprosy.*

Numbers 12:1–11

Now, while Scripture is silent on this, I imagine this must have been a terrible blow to Moses' heart. Aaron was his brother. They had been joyfully reunited in the desert. They had stood before Pharaoh. Miriam was his sister. She was the one who had watched him float in the Nile. She had approached Pharaoh's daughter for the family. She was a prophetess who had danced and sang with praise when God delivered them at the Red Sea (Exodus 15:20).

And now they stood against him . . .

Even when we think things are clear and understood, there can be problems. However, as church leaders, we should attempt to avoid as many of these seemingly inevitable problems can. This is principally done as we define the expectations for each role in the church. Which of the following should come first?

a. Judging whether or not the task is being accomplished well?

b. Determining what the task is?

The answer to this question is obvious, yet rarely is the concept accurately applied. Whether we are talking about paid professionals or part-time volunteers, it is very important to define the ministry that is expected to be accomplished. We all have different expectations concerning what it takes to successfully accomplish every task. If roles are not clearly defined, we have set at the very least a course for frustration and at the worst complete failure.

To assure ministry clarification, each worker must:

- *Know his task and believe it to be important*
- *Understand and support the objective of the overall program*
- *Be conscious of his relationship to other workers*
- *Be free from an atmosphere of intimidation*
- *Have a significant role in the group process*
- *Be alert to his responsibility toward maintaining a spirit of unity and community in the group.*[2]

Many people in the church operate at sub-par levels simply because they don't know what is expected of them. If we clearly define the task and the accompanying expectations for its success at the time that the task

---

2. Gangel, Kenneth, *Feeding and Leading*. Baker Books, 2000.

is assigned, most people will be very happy to work hard to get the task done. We want to know what our ministry task is so that we can be sure when we are doing it well.

In the first part of this section, you were asked to list a few structural responsibilities and the person linked to each. As you are moving forward to define leadership roles, consider three basic factors. (This will also be part of the Action Steps later.)

1. Does the previous list truly define needed leadership roles? If not, what would need to be added or subtracted?
2. Based on the list of roles that are needed, clearly define the tasks that each position would set about to accomplish. (Include in this list the length of service required to accomplish the role. Is it permanent or short-term?)
3. Define the structure that will be used to oversee these positions. Begin at the top (pastor or church board) and work your way down. (Or begin at the bottom and work your way up! Who is in the position of serving each group?)

WHAT IS THE RELATIONSHIP BETWEEN SPIRITUAL GIFTS AND CHURCH EFFECTIVENESS?

As we discussed earlier, a key premise for moving forward as a church is this: *God does not ask the church to do anything that He has not already given it the resources to accomplish.* We should therefore organize efficiently to get the most out of the resources that God has provided. Spiritual gifts must now be addressed.

> *The Christian leader understands that he functions in order to facilitate the ministry of others. He does what he must do in order that they may do what God has called them to do.*[3]

One of the greatest responsibilities of the leaders in the church is to help the congregation to find their place of ministry. One of the greatest failures of leaders in the church is to fail to help individuals discover their spiritual gifts so that they may fulfill a specific role in the church.

---

3. Ibid.

> *It was He who gave some to be apostles, some to be prophets, some to be evangelists, and some to be pastors and teachers, to prepare God's people for works of service, so that the body of Christ may be built up until we all reach unity in the faith and in the knowledge of the Son of God and become mature, attaining to the whole measure of the fullness of Christ.*
>
> Ephesians 4:11–13

In order to facilitate this discovery and ministry placement, it is sometimes helpful to consider this relationship between giftedness and effectiveness in light of three categories:

- *Discovery*: How will we help our members to discover their Spiritual and Ministry Gifts?

- *Development*: How will we equip our members to fully make use of their Spiritual and Ministry Gifts?

- *Deployment*: What system will we use to assure that our members are effectively implementing their gifts?

In terms of Discovery, there are several tools that leaders can use to explore and "test" members in the areas of Spiritual and Ministry Gifts. Because of the differences in denominations, one of the first places should be to solicit the help from your denominational headquarters. There are also many books and supplemental resources available to do quick, simple assessments as well as more thorough examinations. The simplest method is to just ask! Often the parallels between a person's likes and giftedness are remarkably similar (almost to the extent of pointing to a Divine Designer!).

Once these gifts have been discovered (or affirmed), the leaders must see that the gifts are developed. In which ways may a person with such gifts serve in the church? In which ways may that person serve the church outside of the physical walls? The shepherds in the church must tend to the care of their flock's needs and help them to grow spiritually and practically in service.

Would a doctor go through years of study and training and then retire to sit on the beach without ever seeing a patient? Of course not! The training and pursuit of the call is what drove them to the countless hours of reading books and interning at hospitals and clinics. In the same manner, a person who has been awakened into service should never sit back and wait for ministry opportunities to stumble into their pew.

Leaders must make sure those gifted are deployed into service and receive continuing discipleship as they move forward. Don't start a fire and then ignore the flames!

WHY IS IT IMPORTANT TO HAVE A SYSTEM FOR MOVING PEOPLE THROUGH THE DISCIPLESHIP PROCESS?

Let's talk about Joshua for awhile. We first meet this "aide" to Moses in Exodus 17.

> *The Amalekites came and attacked the Israelites at Rephidim. Moses said to Joshua, "Choose some of our men and go out to fight the Amalekites. Tomorrow I will stand on top of the hill with the staff of God in my hands."*
>
> Exodus 17:8–9

For Moses to have designated this task to Joshua, he must have already demonstrated some leadership characteristics. As the battle ensued, we see the nation of Israel winning as long as the staff of God was lifted up. To Joshua, this must have been an early demonstration that GOD was the one who had all the power.

Joshua then attends to Moses as he meets with God on Mt. Sinai.

> *Then Moses set out with Joshua his aide, and Moses went up on the mountain of God. He said to the elders, "Wait here for us until we come back to you. Aaron and Hur are with you, and anyone involved in a dispute can go to them."*
>
> Ex 24:13–14

Joshua returned with Moses as the people in the camp were worshipping the golden calf. He was a witness to God's wrath being poured out on the sinning Israelites. Again, this was a powerful testimony to Joshua of the consequences of sin and rebellion. Personally, I think this was probably very influential in Joshua's life as he grew spiritually. Look closely at this next verse.

> *The LORD would speak to Moses face to face, as a man speaks with his friend. Then Moses would return to the camp, but his young aide Joshua son of Nun did not leave the tent.*
>
> Exodus 33:11

Normally, I'd stop at the first sentence of that verse. Imagine—speaking to God face to face as you would speak to a friend! I can't imagine Moses ever returning to camp. But, as a leader, Moses knew he had to return to the people. He'd seen what had happened when he left to ascend Mt. Sinai.

But that verse also tells us that Joshua did not leave the tent. In reading a few commentators, some speculation made me laugh a bit. One deduced that Joshua stayed in case God said something while Moses was gone. (What? God wouldn't have known Moses wasn't there?) Another thought he was always ready for Moses to return and that was the best place to wait.

I think I agree with those who thought Joshua did not *want* to leave. The Tent of Meeting was the place of God's Presence. Why would he want to be anywhere else?

Joshua, Moses' eventual successor, spent time with Moses. He spent time with God. He was immersed in the mission and so obedient to it, that he (and Caleb) stood strong in the face of the enemy while everyone else chose to run (Numbers 13).

* * * * *

The reason I bring all of this up is to encourage you to truly think about disciple-making. What are you doing to help people grow spiritually? What are you doing to equip today's leaders and the leaders of tomorrow?

Without an intentional system in place, people will drift into church and drift right back out. An effort must be made to assimilate these individuals into the life of the church. To meld some teachings from Rick Warren and Bill Hull, we can look as someone is moved through the process to spiritual maturity.

The Lost (Lookers) come to belief through evangelism and the call of God upon their hearts (John 1:35–51; Mark 3:13). The New Believer becomes a Learner as the truths of Scripture are imprinted upon the heart (Mark 4:33–34). This Rooted Disciple is transformed into a Laborer as they begin service to the King (Mark 3:13–14). The Servant is then "employed" by the Master for work in the Kingdom (Mark 6:7–13).

This is a *process*. With some excellent exceptions, many churches are either becoming "Lost-focused" or "Maintainers." In simple terms, the church either evangelizes or accepts the "movers" and "hoppers." In either case, if there is no guidance, once a person has become a member, that individual either seeks out a place of comfortable involvement or blends into the shadows. As time moves on, they either become entrenched in their place of involvement or drift out the door from their former place in the shadows.

Perhaps the greatest example of this can be seen through the story of Willow Creek church near Chicago. For years, it was lauded as "the" church of growth. It launched the "seeker sensitive" movement. However, in 2007, Bill Hybels related in the book Reveal:

> *Among the findings: nearly one out of every four people at Willow Creek were stalled in their spiritual growth or dissatisfied with the church—and many of them were considering leaving.*[4]

The conclusion? While they had invested years and years of effort and thousands upon thousands of dollars, they had failed in making disciples. Yes, many had made professions of faith, but they were spiritually starving. They kept nibbling around the crust of the sandwich while never taking a bite to enjoy the real taste.

Lay Renewal has encouraged and equipped church leaders for outreach *and* spiritual growth for more than five decades. We have clearly seen that as people believe they are being discipled through an intentional process of spiritual growth and ministry connection, they will feel firmly attached to the church. As they understand the plan and what is expected of them regarding their ongoing learning and ministry involvement, they will know that they are part of God's plan for the church. Church leaders—as shepherds—are responsible for the spiritual growth and nurture of their "sheep." This process will assure that you are accomplishing God's commission to make disciples. Help your people understand *from the beginning* that your church is serious about disciple making. This attitude will please far more people than it will offend.

> *Church leaders may stir up opposition in the church in two ways. The first is by obeying God and leading the church according to God's agenda. This creates a great deal of friction. The other way is to be passive and allow the church to stagnate. This method causes the congregation to criticize the leaders for their lack of leadership.*

---

4. Hawkins, Greg L. and Cally Parkinson, *Reveal*. Willow Creek Resources, 2007.

Either way, leadership faces opposition, so why not make your opposition count?[5]

---

5. Hull, Bill, *Disciple Making Church*. Baker Books, 1998.

Action Steps:

1. Does your church have a top-down or a bottom-up structure? Are the job descriptions of those in place dependent upon serving, leading or a combination of both?

2. Study John 13:1–17. What effect does Jesus model of servant leadership play into your understanding of your role in the church?

3. Refer back to the section on defining Leadership Roles in the church. What sort of structure does your church currently have in place? Define the roles, positions and structure. Organize a chart to show the responsibilities of staff and volunteers.

4. Evaluate the awareness and training available for the discovery, development and deployment of Spiritual and Ministry Gifts in your church. Create a test (or obtain one) for evaluating the giftedness of the members of your church. How then can you develop and deploy the results of the test?

_____

_____

_____

_____

5. Hold a foot-washing service in the church. Allow the pastor to wash the feet of the leadership team and then have that team wash the feet of members. Although there is often *a lot* of hesitation in the church, this event can have a powerful effect on church members. (As an additional help, you may want to consider a study on "feet" in the Bible. From Genesis to Malachi and Matthew to Revelation, "feet" serve as powerful imagery for many different aspects of faith and life!)

Tier 3

Direction

Therefore, in the present case I advise you: Leave these men alone! Let them go! For if their purpose or activity is of human origin, it will fail. But if it is from God, you will not be able to stop these men; you will only find yourselves fighting against God.

Acts 5:38–39

At this point in our journey, the summit is in sight. Mission should be set and the leaders should have a great understanding of Unity. Components of Communication and Structure are now firmly set as we enter an important switchback—Direction.

In order to understand Direction, it is crucial that we strive to grow deeper and deeper in our connection with God through the study of His Word and prayer. God will work through us to reveal how He wants His plan to be accomplished. As a compass always points to true north, we must seek His direction in all things in order to achieve real success.

How do you define "success?" To be blunt, in the church, success is defined by God and God alone. As Gamaliel addressed the Sanhedrin in the fifth chapter of Acts, he wisely cautioned everyone to let God ultimately determine the outcome of the actions and teachings of the apostles. As weak, sinful human beings, we are prone to error. If we persist in fighting God's will, like the Sanhedrin, we will find ourselves struggling in vain.

And, as we addressed in the switchback of Unity, we must be vigilant to address any issues that arise. These must be seized as opportunities to grow and strengthen the Body. As we see in Acts, the number of disciples rapidly increased. This was a wonderful blessing for the early church as they continued to see God moving among them. However, this growth led to conflict.

> *In those days when the number of disciples was increasing, the Grecian Jews among them complained against the Hebraic Jews because their widows were being overlooked in the daily distribution of food. So the Twelve gathered all the disciples together and said, "It would not be right for us to neglect the ministry of the word of God in order to wait on tables. Brothers, choose seven men from among you who are known to be full of the Spirit and wisdom. We will turn this responsibility over to them and will give our attention to prayer and the ministry of the word."*

Acts 6:1–4

The apostles did not fight or argue. The Twelve kept their focus. Their focus was to pray and share the Word. Through this event, not only did they remain focused, they seized the opportunity to allow seven others to exercise the gifts that God had given them!

Serving in and through the church is not easy. It requires focus and discipline to remain obedient to God while still demonstrating love, grace and mercy to those struggling with life. This is why our strength must be in Christ rather than ourselves. This is why we must seek to focus our efforts and endeavors in His ministry rather than our programs. This is why we seek His vision.

8

Vision

Finding the Blueprint

Prior to 2005, my eyesight fell in the realm of technically being considered legally blind without corrective measures. This obviously presented some challenges—including getting up in the morning! If I woke up before my alarm, I would have to pull my face close to the giant numbers to determine the time. When I took out my contacts at night, I often had to do a search for my glasses. It would drive my wife crazy because I would walk around in the dark. I didn't see a point in turning on the lights if I couldn't see!

And then—*Laser Eye Surgery*! It was amazing to wake up the next morning and be able to see perfectly. If you haven't experienced a change like that, the joy of being able to see clearly is simply too difficult to put into words.

What does this have to do with the Church and vision? The best way I can connect the two is to tell a story . . .

Several years ago, I was a few months into a consultation with a church. It had not been an especially exciting few months. "*Beating your head against a wall*" seemed a fairly apt description. Things were stalled. Impatience was growing and so were the arguments. But then we had a "light-bulb moment." An elderly gentleman stood up in the middle of a church-wide discussion meeting and tearfully said, "I really don't care what we do. All I know is my grandson won't come to church with me and I want that to change."

Can you guess the impact that had on the group? From that point on, the discussion moved forward rather than in circles.

Our Biblical model for vision is a man whose resume looked rather simple.

> *I was cupbearer to the king.*
>
> Nehemiah 1:11c

In modern vernacular, we might assume that the man was a waiter. While that may be true in a sense, in Old Testament times, the cupbearer was the person to whom the king looked when he wanted something to drink. While not being exactly the most difficult job in the world, many believe the cupbearer had an additional duty as the taste-tester. Before the king would take a drink, the cupbearer would take a sip. If he did not die, the king knew it would be safe to drink from the cup. The cupbearer would therefore be a very special person to the king and would hold a high degree of trust.

How did the man who was a cupbearer become the leader who was chiefly responsible for coordinating the effort to rebuild the walls of Jerusalem in only fifty-two days? He was a man of God who believed in prayer. (While we will focus on a few aspects of Nehemiah's life in this chapter, two other books present excellent insights on this man of God: *Visioneering* by Andy Stanley or *Hand Me Another Brick* by Charles Swindoll.) Let's take a look behind the scenes.

> *Hanani, one of my brothers, came from Judah with some other men, and I questioned them about the Jewish remnant that survived the exile, and also about Jerusalem. They said to me, "Those who survived the exile and are back in the province are in great trouble and disgrace. The wall of Jerusalem is broken down, and its gates have been burned with fire. When I heard these things, I sat down and wept. For some days I mourned and fasted and prayed before the God of heaven.*
>
> Nehemiah 1:2–4

Although there is not sufficient time to digress into great detail regarding the walls, suffice it to say that without them, the Israelites were hardly a people. They were defenseless and open to bullying from all those around them. Nehemiah understood the implications immediately and was so torn by it that he could only sit, weep and pray for several days.

After this he jumped into action. He called in the army to defend Jerusalem. He gathered the king's personal construction crew and set them to work. He . . .

OK—that's not exactly what happened.

What did he do? He continued to pray and seek God's guidance for helping the people in Jerusalem. *Four months* later, he had the opportunity to plead his case before the king. When that opportunity came, he was ready to act (after another quick arrow prayer to heaven!)

Nehemiah understood there was a problem (v. 2–3). Nehemiah was motivated to do something about the problem (v. 4). Nehemiah reached out in obedience to the ultimate Source of help for a solution to the problem (v. 4–11). Nehemiah then received a vision from God for rebuilding the walls around Jerusalem.

I am going to have to ask you to grant me a little latitude at this point. How can I say with such confidence that God gave Nehemiah a vision when Scripture does not explicitly tell us this? I think it was a God-given vision because of the response that Nehemiah received from the king, the subsequent response from the people of Jerusalem and the ultimate success of the project. Given the enormity of the task and the impossible odds, success was impossible unless God's hand was upon the project.

When seeking to build or rebuild the framework of any church, we must likewise feel confident in God's hand upon the church and the plans we are making. A vision from God will be revealed. The vision must be birthed from a motivation of loving appreciation to the Creator and Redeemer. The vision must be prepared out of obedience to the calling of God upon a particular church. The vision with God's hand upon it will succeed even in the feeblest of hands simply because He wills it to succeed.

> *Where there is no vision, the people perish; but he that keepeth the law, happy is he.*
> Proverbs 29:18 (KJV)

Sacrificial commitment to a cause requires clear focus as to the intent of the cause. We must believe that what we are doing is significant if we are going to become fully involved.

> *After this, the word of the LORD came to Abram in a vision: "Do not be afraid, Abram. I am your shield, your very great reward."*
>
> Genesis 15:1

God provides the vision and the means to carry it out.

> *Paul and his companions traveled throughout the region of Phrygia and Galatia, having been kept by the Holy Spirit from preaching the word in the province of Asia. When they came to the border of Mysia, they tried to enter Bithynia, but the Spirit of Jesus would not allow them to. So they passed by Mysia and went down to Troas. During the night Paul had a vision of a man of Macedonia standing and begging him, "Come over to Macedonia and help us." After Paul had seen the vision, we got ready at once to leave for Macedonia, concluding that God had called us to preach the gospel to them.*
>
> Acts 16:6–10

As we continue to focus our attention on God, He will keep our vision on track. He plants the seed, waters the seed and helps the seed to grow. We just need to make sure we are attached to the vine and praying to the vinedresser.

GUIDING PRINCIPLE

Vision for ministry is a clear mental image of a preferable future imparted by God to His chosen servants and is based upon an accurate understanding of God, self and circumstances.

—George Barna

THE CHALLENGE OF LEADERSHIP

Leaders in the church are obviously greatly impacted by the component of vision. As I've mentioned, the movie, *Braveheart*, presents a powerful example when William Wallace turns around the deserting troops with a bold, impassioned speech. The men are called to action and probable death not out of duty, but rather a vision of what their lives will be like if they do *not* fight. A good vision will likewise become a powerful engine that influences everything that the church does. Effective churches must have a clear vision for ministry.

It is first necessary that we define and differentiate the meaning behind words like purpose, mission, vision, objectives and strategies. After we define those words for the purpose of this study, we will then look at the following key questions.

- What is our mission as Christians?
- What is God's purpose for the Church?
- Why is a specific vision important for each individual church?
- What are the benefits of a vision statement?
- What is the role of church leadership in determining God's vision for our church?
- What are the five vital dimensions of planning?

Exploring the answers to these questions and then working through the exercises will help both you and the other leaders in your church to determine your church's vision by understanding where you are, who you are and who God is.

WHAT'S THE DIFFERENCE?

Because our experiences and backgrounds can be so varied, there are many definitions to describe the following terms. While there will be some difference in perceptions, it is important that your leadership team comes to consensus as to your church's understanding of the definition of the terms. Everyone must be on the same page regarding your unique understanding of the concepts. For the sake of clarity here, we will define our key concepts as follows:

Mission: We define mission as the specific yet overarching task to which a person or group of people has been assigned. For your church, it is God's plan or, as it is sometimes called, your *purpose*. In the architecture that makes up the model we use in this book, it is mission that lays the Godly foundation. Mission includes motivation, obedience and attitude. It is the spiritual environment and the undergirding of all that you do as a church. Mission (purpose) answer the question, "Why do we exist?"

Vision: God's vision for your church lays out what you believe God is calling you to be in the future. Every church will have a different vision for why they exist depending on their specific circumstances. The unique vision of your church is determined by the uniqueness of the people of your individual church. The "Divine Design" of each individual serves to make up the total personality of the church.

Objectives: Once you have ascertained what God's vision is for your church, establish objectives or "action areas," which prioritize "how" you believe you are going to accomplish your vision. These are short term and long term. Your objectives translate your abstract ideas into concrete plans. Another word to include and expand the meaning of our understanding of objectives is "goals."

Strategies: Once you have established your objectives (or goals), you must begin to lay out the plan that specifically states how you are going to accomplish those objectives. Strategies include specific detail as you document clearly defined and measurable plans. These details should include the establishment of time lines and finances. These are crucial to help you determine the pace of your actions.

WHAT IS OUR MISSION AS CHRISTIANS?

Nehemiah's prayer to God began in this way:

> "O LORD, God of heaven, the great and awesome God, who keeps his covenant of love with those who love him and obey his commands, let your ear be attentive and your eyes open to hear the prayer your servant is praying before you day and night for your servants, the people of Israel. I confess the sins we Israelites, including myself and my father's house, have committed against you. We have acted very wickedly toward you. We have not obeyed the commands, decrees and laws you gave your servant Moses."

Nehemiah 1:5–7

Nehemiah didn't whine. He didn't complain. God was *not* at fault. His commands, decrees and laws had been perfectly clear. If the people had obeyed them, they would have enjoyed God's abundant blessings. Instead of following that path, Nehemiah, his father's house and the nation of Israel had acted wickedly and sinned against God.

Rather than try to think up a list that defines our mission as Christians, let's boil it down to the essence: *Be a Christian*!

Can it really be that simple? Yes.

That doesn't mean it will be easy. The world is a fallen and sinful place. But a Christian is a Christ-follower (Acts 9:25–26).

When we follow someone, we seek to become like them. We are to be like Christ. We will not be perfect, but we are to strive each day to take up our cross and follow Him. Since we have been motivated by the love of Christ and we have been adopted as children of our Heavenly Father, we are to be obedient to His calling in our lives. Our lives as believers are to be different than the lives of non-believers. Christianity is not simply a concept of what we are. It is an all-encompassing *model of what we are to be*. We are to be living lives in a manner worthy of our calling. There are generally accepted moral principles of what this means. However, the specifics will be broken down for each individual Christian as he or she determines the purpose, vision, objectives and strategies God has for them. This is done in light of God's Word.

WHAT IS GOD'S PURPOSE FOR THE CHURCH?

"Why are we here?" is a crucial question that must be asked and answered on an ongoing basis. In the corporate world, the development of purpose statements became a highly emphasized endeavor in the nineties. The concept was a very valid one. If those working in the organization understood their purpose as part of something larger than themselves, they would be encouraged to extend themselves for their own betterment as well as that of those around them. "Present thinking" became intertwined with "future thinking."

Similarly, the church has recognized the value of having a purpose statement for the same reasons. The difference in the case of the church is that it is not necessary to create a purpose statement! Jesus himself determined the purpose for the church:

> *Go and make disciples of all nations.*
>
> Matthew 28:19a

Every church that is true to their calling as the Body of Christ should embrace Christ's commission as the basis for their own specific purpose statement. *If making disciples is not your basic reason for existence as a church, then you are not accomplishing the main task set out for you as a church.*

A purpose statement, when created for your specific church, will give your people a rallying call. When asked, they should be able to succinctly state your purpose. It should be easy to remember and recite. Below are some examples of actual purpose statements.

> *To evangelize, edify, equip and exalt.*
>
> *To know Him and to make Him known.*
>
> *To reach the lost, teach the found and make disciples of the Lord Jesus Christ.*
>
> *To save the lost and strengthen the saved to live bold and courageous lives of Christian witness before a non-believing world.*
>
> *To worship God, disciple believers, build community within the church, pray for direction, forgiveness and power, and extend compassion to the needy.*

Can you see the uniting theme in all of these good purpose statements? "To make disciples"

WHY IS VISION IMPORTANT FOR INDIVIDUAL CHURCHES?

> *Successful churches have a clear understanding of God's vision for them. Not the vision of the pastor or the strategic planning committee or the denomination, but God's vision for the church captured through significant amounts of study, prayer and counsel. The vision drives the church to action. The vision becomes the filter through which all church activities are evaluated. Activities that coincide with the vision are pursued, and those that fall outside the parameters of the vision are rejected.*
>
> —George Barna

It is impossible to embrace a common vision and engage in its accomplishments if that vision is not universally understood and promoted. The downfall of many churches is mixed agendas and expectations as to what the church is trying to be about.

How did Nehemiah model an effective vision for the people? He told them simply.

> *Then I said to them, "You see the trouble we are in: Jerusalem lies in ruins, and its gates have been burned with fire. Come, let us rebuild the wall of Jerusalem, and we will no longer be in disgrace."*

Nehemiah 2:17

Isn't that easy to understand? In order to stop being a disgrace, the people of Jerusalem needed to rally together and rebuild a visible sign of their shame. Did that vision capture the hearts of the people? The next verse tells us:

> *I also told them about the gracious hand of my God upon me and what the king had said to me. They replied, "Let us start rebuilding." So they began this good work.*

Nehemiah 2:18

It is clear that they accepted the vision. They started rebuilding. They understood the simplicity of the task at hand. While that seems too easy, I hope you caught the first part of that verse as well. Nehemiah encouraged them by telling them what God had already done. Let's stop for a minute. In order to fully appreciate the message, put yourself in the context.

Imagine: You are part of the remnant in Jerusalem. You were not found "worthy" to be taken into captivity but instead were left to farm the land and send tribute to the king. From reading the ways in which Sanballat the Horonite, Tobiah the Ammonite official and Geshem the Arab mocked the rebuilding (see verse 19), I think it is safe to assume morale was fairly low. But now—*hope*! God's hand is once again with you.

Church effectiveness is dependent on all the members of the church working toward the accomplishment of the same agendas. These agendas must be bathed in prayer as the Holy Spirit washes over them. Vision statements clarify a more specific God-given direction for the church.

As a brief exercise, consider the following actual vision statements. Try to pull out from them a description of the path these churches see God leading them on. Is it clear? Is it memorable? Does it paint a picture of the future?

> *To attract families by developing an extensive, excellent program of spiritual and relational opportunities for children and youth. The church will focus on family issues as a means to facilitate spiritual wholeness.*
>
> *To reach out to the greater metropolitan area toward raising up four new churches by 2000, to demonstrate God's love, creativity and power by caring for people working in cooperation with other ministries to reach the region for Christ.*
>
> *To equip professionals in New York City to impact their web of relationships, focusing on reaching non-Christians through cell groups and market place ministries that address urban needs.*

WHAT ARE THE BENEFITS OF A VISION STATEMENT?

When we reflect on the rebuilding of the walls, it is possible to think that it was a fairly easy process. Nehemiah did have the support of the king. However, don't read over it too quickly. The people faced strong opposition from other local political leaders. The Israelites were insulted, threatened and ridiculed. This was a spiritual and emotional battle.

> *Hear us, O our God, for we are despised. Turn their insults back on their own heads. Give them over as plunder in a land of captivity. Do not cover up their guilt or blot out their sins from your sight, for they have thrown insults in the face of the builders. So we rebuilt the wall till all of it reached half its height, for the people worked with all their heart.*
>
> Nehemiah 4:4–6

As churches seek to move forward for God's glory, they will face opposition. It may be from a member of the community. It may be from another church. It may even be from a member of the church itself. However, it is important to keep focused on what God is doing through you. Keep focused on the vision God has given you to reach people for His glory.

A shared vision provides motivation and direction for obedience to God. It offers a practical outlet. A shared vision becomes the driving force of your church. It assures commonality of purpose. Time and again, churches that have lost vision or failed to communicate that vision have lost members or closed their doors. It is easy to see a church in maintenance mode because its members are lethargic about their roles and unwilling to serve.

In his book, *The Master's Plan for Making Disciples*, Win Arn lists the following benefits of vision statements:

- Unify the members of the church
- Provide motivation for action
- Establish a basis for accountability
- Give assurance that you are doing God's work, not busy work
- Give the church an overall direction
- Define what the church does and does not do
- Alleviate false guilt and provide a basis for measuring accomplishments[1]

After reading over that list, take a few minutes to go back and reflect on each one. Does your church have a clear and compelling vision? Does it achieve each point? Is there a way you can strengthen it? Is there a way you can communicate it better?

In his book, *The Disciple Making Church*, Bill Hull summarized it this way:

> *The church operates at low efficiency because too few work. Everything the church needs resides in the undisciplined body members, but neglectful leaders have not provided the vision. So much is not done by so many who could do it. Well over 50% of the average congregation is a ministry wasteland. People go unchallenged and untrained, unused and unfulfilled.* [2]

WHAT IS THE ROLE OF CHURCH LEADERSHIP IN DETERMINING GOD'S VISION FOR THE CHURCH?

In the last section, I mentioned that you might face opposition from *inside* your church. Do you think this is possible? Unfortunately, it is a rather harsh reality of this world. Even Nehemiah had to deal with problems among the people.

The rebuilding of the walls—even though it only took 52 days—exacted a toll on the people. Because they were so focused on the work, other things were set aside. In addition, it appears that problems that had

---

1. Arn, Win and Charles Win, *Master's Plan for Making Disciples*. Baker Books, 1998.
2. Hull, Bill, *Disciple Making Church*. Baker Books, 1998.

developed *prior* to the rebuilding came to light. (The increased tension may have played a part in this occurring.)

The charges levied by the people were serious. They were starving and unable to feed their families. They were borrowing money and being charged interest by their fellow Israelites. Some were even forced to sell their children into slavery. Nehemiah did not shy away from this controversy or let it distract him from the vision. He reflected and acted immediately.

> *When I heard their outcry and these charges, I was very angry. I pondered them in my mind and then accused the nobles and officials. I told them, "You are exacting usury from your own countrymen!" So I called together a large meeting to deal with them and said: "As far as possible, we have bought back our Jewish brothers who were sold to the Gentiles. Now you are selling your brothers, only for them to be sold back to us!" They kept quiet, because they could find nothing to say.*
>
> *So I continued, "What you are doing is not right. Shouldn't you walk in the fear of our God to avoid the reproach of our Gentile enemies? I and my brothers and my men are also lending the people money and grain. But let the exacting of usury stop! Give back to them immediately their fields, vineyards, olive groves and houses, and also the usury you are charging them-the hundredth part of the money, grain, new wine and oil." "We will give it back," they said. "And we will not demand anything more from them. We will do as you say." Then I summoned the priests and made the nobles and officials take an oath to do what they had promised. I also shook out the folds of my robe and said, "In this way may God shake out of his house and possessions every man who does not keep this promise. So may such a man be shaken out and emptied!" At this the whole assembly said, "Amen," and praised the LORD. And the people did as they had promised.*
>
> Nehemiah 5:6–13

How did Nehemiah deal with the problem?

1. He listened.
2. He reflected.
3. He called the people together.
4. He told them the problem.
5. He proposed a solution.

This is model for conflict resolution is an excellent method for every leader to embrace! It also is a clarion call for leaders to be actively engaged in their roles in the vision process.

Vision is from God. God has a very specific plan for each local church. God has provided your church with visionary leaders. Your pastor may believe that he has been called as a visionary leader in your church. However, according to a recent George Barna survey, the vast majority of pastors do not consider visionary leadership to be their primary spiritual attribute. If this is the case, the necessity of the leadership team to work together to ascertain God's vision for your church is even more apparent.

That said, we must recognize that it is the responsibility of the senior pastor to champion God's vision for His church. The pastor must be passionately attached to the vision of the church if it is to capture the attention of the congregation.

It is also appropriate and necessary for the entire leadership team to explore the possibilities of God's vision for the church. The vision should be birthed out of prayer, diligence and commitment to God. The leaders should be putting forth the vision and incorporating it within the ministries they oversee.

WHAT ARE THE FIVE VITAL DIMENSIONS OF PLANNING?

There are five vital dimensions that church leaders must understand when they begin to work through a vision casting and master planning process. Churches operate differently than any other gathering of people. We are a community that is to operate with a different set of rules than those used by the secular world. Intentionally taking advantage of the benefits of working within our unique church environments will make the planning easier and more effective. The five dimensions are as follows:

Prayer: The church has been given a mighty tool to discern God's will and accomplish His purposes. If we forego the spiritual resource that has been given to us through the power of prayer, we eliminate our greatest advantage in working together as the community of God. [For further study, reflect on Nehemiah 1:4, 11]

Biblical Perspective: There is no reason for Christians to struggle with setting up procedures and bylaws. We have already been given a spiritual set of bylaws and a standard of procedures (structure) in the Bible. Throughout its pages, God has exemplified situational threats and decisions we might face. Master planning must therefore be accomplished based on a Biblical perspective. All considerations and plans in the church should be weighted according to God's dealings with man as depicted in the Bible. [For further study, reflect on Nehemiah 5:1—7:3.]

Dialogue: Talk! It is critical that much time be given to discussing the issues that will impact the entire membership of the church. The way that we go about communicating with one another will greatly impact our success. God has called us to be unified in thought and spirit. As we respect others more than ourselves, we will operate with great effectiveness. [For further study, reflect on Nehemiah 2:2, 17–18.]

Ownership: As members of your congregation are offered the opportunity to become a part of the planning process, they will support it. Again—the church is a body. All of the parts are important and necessary to healthy functioning of the body as a whole. Gather information and participation through surveys or town hall meetings. Including all the members of the congregation in the process will help them to own and be responsibile for implementation of God's vision. [For further study, reflect on Nehemiah 4:14–15.]

Consensus: Support for plans and actions should be derived through consensus building, rather than elections. When votes are taken, there are winners and losers. When people are lovingly convinced as to the benefit and spiritual directive of our plans, they can wholeheartedly commit to them. Our main objective is unity in thought rather than division of opinions. [For further study, reflect on Nehemiah 2:18.]

THE IMPORTANCE OF CASTING VISION

Early in His ministry on earth, Jesus was standing by Lake Gennesaret teaching the people. Because of the size of the crowd, He climbed into Simon Peter's boat and taught from there. When He had finished speaking, He did something very interesting. He told Simon to go fishing again. Not only did He tell Simon to go fishing, Jesus told him that he was going to catch something.

> *"Put out into deep water, and let down the nets for a catch." Simon answered, "Master, we've worked hard all night and haven't caught anything. But because you say so, I will let down the nets. When they had done so, they caught such a large number of fish that their nets began to break. So they signaled their partners in the other boat to come and help them, and they came and filled both boats so full that they began to sink.*
>
> Luke 5:4–7

Obviously, Simon didn't think going fishing was such a great idea. After all, they worked all night and then they listened to Jesus teach. But Simon follows the command because he recognized the authority and vision of the One speaking to him. They reaped a great reward. And what happened next?

> *When Simon Peter saw this, he fell at Jesus' knees and said, "Go away from me, Lord; I am a sinful man!" For he and all his companions were astonished at the catch of fish they had taken, and so were James and John, the sons of Zebedee, Simon's partners. Then Jesus said to Simon, "Don't be afraid; from now on you will catch men." So they pulled their boats up on shore, left everything and followed Him.*
>
> Luke 5:8–11

The conviction that we are following Jesus Christ in our actions should drive us to fervently undertake carrying out the mission that He has given us. "Go and make disciples." No exercise that you undertake in your church is more important than taking the time to discern God's vision to carry out the mission He has given your church. Communicate that vision and get on with accomplishing it.

Action Steps:

1. Vision casting is a process. It is a process that will have a major impact on your church for many years into the future. Needless to say, it cannot be accomplished through a short exercise. However, use these small steps to begin thinking and praying about the vision process. Remember the definition of vision as stated by George Barna: "*A clear mental image of a preferable future imparted by God to His chosen servants, and based upon an accurate understanding of God, self and circumstances.*"

2. Spend some personal time in prayer for clarity from God as to the future vision of your church. Write down a few of the specific elements that might be a part of your church's future vision.

   _____

   _____

   _____

   _____

   _____

3. Form groups of 4 to 8 people and pray corporately for clarity from God as to the future vision of your church. As a group, take another 10 to 15 minutes to develop a list of specific elements that might be a part of your church's future vision.

4. Schedule a time of praying and fasting for your entire church to seek God's direction for your church. (Make sure you take time to study and teach the Scriptural dynamics of prayer and fasting prior to scheduling the event.) Help your congregation to understand

that developing a master plan will be of critical importance to the effective future of your church. Pray for unity and enthusiasm as God reveals His vision for your church to your pastor and leaders.

5. Develop a plan to develop a plan. Begin an intentional process as a leadership team to set the course for your church's future. Taking the time to get an accurate understanding of your congregation's current perceptions about your present ministry effectiveness is an excellent starting point.

Conclusion

(or is it?)

ABRAHAM WAS NOT THE first person who started to go to the Promised Land.

> *This is the account of Terah. Terah became the father of Abram, Nahor and Haran. And Haran became the father of Lot. While his father Terah was still alive, Haran died in Ur of the Chaldeans, in the land of his birth. Abram and Nahor both married. The name of Abram's wife was Sarai, and the name of Nahor's wife was Milcah; she was the daughter of Haran, the father of both Milcah and Iscah. Now Sarai was barren; she had no children. Terah took his son Abram, his grandson Lot son of Haran, and his daughter-in-law Sarai, the wife of his son Abram, and together they set out from Ur of the Chaldeans to go to Canaan. But when they came to Haran, they settled there. Terah lived 205 years, and he died in Haran.*
>
> Genesis 11:27–32

Many people skim quickly over this passage in Genesis. Abram (Abraham) is the one remembered as the Patriarch and we are anxious to get to the details of his story. However, Terah was actually the one who originally set out to go to Canaan.

Why did he stop in Haran? Scripture is silent. But we do know that Terah was not a follower of the one true God.

> *Joshua said to all the people, "This is what the LORD, the God of Israel, says: 'Long ago your forefathers, including Terah the father of Abraham and Nahor, lived beyond the River and worshiped other gods. But I took your father Abraham from the land beyond the River and led him throughout Canaan and gave him many descendants.'"*
>
> Joshua 24:2–3

In Genesis chapter 12, God called Abram out of Haran to the Promised Land. God then painted a vision of what was to come. It was a powerful picture of the future with land and descendants as numerous stars in the sky. Abraham moved forward—trusting God's faithfulness.

What will you do?

If vision goes no farther than a statement, it will die. The death may be quick or happen over a longer time period, but it is inevitable. Vision *must* become action.

This intention at the end of this book is not to leave you hanging. You may be wondering what we do with the vision once we have it? That's for another discussion. Our purpose here is to guide you to the summit and to look at what is before you. It is when you reach this point that you can truly begin to see. What do I mean?

As you drive Highway 70 from eastern Colorado to western Colorado, the topography changes dramatically. On the eastern side of the state, it is incredibly flat. However, as you reach Denver, you are at the base of the Rocky Mountains. It is an impressive sight. If you stop *there*, you are missing the true greatness. Continue up and as you crest the first mountain pass, you see a portion of the vast mountain range before you. If you have never been in awe of the majesty of God's Creation before this point, this is a great place to start!

But the point is this: The same sensation is yours when you know you have *God's* vision in place. It is a time of rejoicing and celebration. It is a time of unity and clarity. It is a time of awe.

Now you have to go forward. Don't stop. Go forward in the direction that God is calling you. Let His vision flow into the ministries of your church as a living and breathing source of strength. Let His vision breathe life into objectives, goals and strategies that shape your outreach to the community and the world.

Lay Renewal Ministries is here to serve and partner with you as you go forward to the *next* summit. The journey has just begun.

Imagine God breathing through your church.

Be visionary.

Imagine the impact.

Be brave.

Dream big.

Be bold.

Do God-sized ministry.

Be alive.

You are the church.

There is no Plan B.

www.ingramcontent.com/pod-product-compliance
Lightning Source LLC
Chambersburg PA
CBHW071435160426
43195CB00013B/1907